Latinos at Work

Career Role Models for Young Adults

Latino Entrepreneurs

● ●

Susan Zannos

Mitchell Lane
PUBLISHERS

PO Box 619
Bear, Delaware 19701

Latinos at Work

Career Role Models for Young Adults

Careers in Community Service

Careers in Education

Careers in Entertainment

Careers in Law and Politics

Careers in the Music Industry

Careers in Publishing and Communications

Careers in Science and Medicine

Careers in Sports

Careers in Technology

Latino Entrepreneurs

Library of Congress Cataloging-In-Publication Data

Zannos, Susan.

Latino Entrepreneurs/ Susan Zannos.

p. cm.—(Latinos at work)

Includes bibliographical references and index.

Summary: Describes what it takes to be a successful entrepreneur, whether starting from scratch or buying an existing business, focusing on the unique experiences of Hispanic Americans through profiles of Latino business owners.

ISBN 1-58415-089-0

1. New business enterprises—Vocational guidance—United States—Juvenile literature. 2. Hispanic American youth—Vocational guidance—Juvenile literature. 3. Success in business—Vocational guidance—United States—Juvenile literature. 4. Entrepreneurship—United States—Juvenile literature. 5. Hispanic American business enterprises—Juvenile literature. 6. Hispanic American businesspeople—Juvenile literature. [1. Business enterprises. 2. Entrepreneurship. 3. Hispanic Americans. 4. Businesspeople. 5. Business—Vocational guidance. 6. Vocational guidance.] I. Title. II. Series.

HD62.5 .Z36 2001

338'.04'0896073—dc21   2001038090

Latino Entrepreneurs

About the Author

Susan Zannos has been a lifelong educator, having taught at all levels, from pre-school to college, in Mexico, Greece, Italy, Russia, and Lithuania, as well as in the United States. She has published a mystery *Trust the Liar* (Walker and Co.) and *Human Types: Essence and the Enneagram* was published by Samuel Weiser in 1997. She has written several books for children, including Paula Abdul and Cesar Chavez (Mitchell Lane). Susan lives in Oxnard, California.

Photo Credits

The photographs in this book were courtesy of the person being profiled.

Acknowledgments

The profiles of success depicted in Part Two were all written from the author's personal interviews. Interviews were conducted as follows: Abraham Garcia- 3/7/01; Oscar Centeno- 3/20/01; Leticia Herrera- 3/24/01; Gabriel Chavez-3/26/01; Esperanza-Porros-Fields-3/26/01; Araceli Mendoza- 3/27/01; John Leaños-4/6/01; Mabel Tinacá- 4/20/01.

Publisher's Note

The careers depicted in this series are by no means all-inclusive. We have tried to show a representation of what is available by industry. Your career center at school or your local library can be of additional help identifying careers we might not have covered. The Web sites mentioned in this book were all active as of the publication date. Because of the fleeting nature of Web enterprises, we cannot guarantee that all sites will be operational when you are reading this book.

Contents

Becoming an Entrepreneur

TABLE OF CONTENTS

"One of the least well known engines of our recent record economic prosperity is the Hispanic entrepreneur." Raul Yzaguirre, President, National Council of La Raza

"The next great American business success story will be a woman . . . and she undoubtedly will be Hispanic." Amy J. Millman, Executive Director, National Women's Business Council

"Hispanics are creating businesses at *three times* the rate of the rest of the population. Latinas are starting new businesses at *four times* that rate. No other group even comes close." Solomon D. Trujillo, Former CEO, U.S. West.

The quotations above, taken from Dr. Mabel Tinjacá's book ¡*Vision!*, reflect a remarkable and unmistakable trend taking place in the economic life of the United States. Businesses owned by Latinos, and especially by Latinas, are increasing, and thriving, at a rate far greater than businesses owned by any other segment of the population. It is of course not possible to discuss all the many types of businesses that an entrepreneur might own, but it is possible to consider some of the methods that people use to become business owners.

Which method you choose will depend on your own abilities, assets, and resources. Starting your own business is frequently the most practical approach, since a surprising number of businesses are begun on a very small scale, sometimes from home and sometimes in the evenings or on weekends while holding another job or going to school.

Another method of business ownership is buying an existing business. You might find yourself in a position to buy a business where you are employed, for example when the owner wants to retire. Or a member of your family may wish to train someone else to run the business. Such an opportunity can have the advantage of allowing you to make a gradual transition to ownership, since you will be dealing with someone with whom you have already established a working relationship, trust, and respect. Furthermore, you will know the business and how it is run.

A third method is franchising, a business strategy that has revolutionized the economy of the United States and is spreading rapidly throughout the world. There are well over 3,000 franchise companies—and these companies account for over one third of all retail sales. There are definite advantages to owning a franchise: the failure rate of this type of business is less than of independent business start-ups, for instance. There are also disadvantages, such as high initial expenses and the necessity of following the rules of the parent company.

Closely related to franchises are network marketing opportunities and dealerships and distributorships, which are the most prevalent businesses in the field of auto sales and gasoline stations (see Spotlight Story on page 14). There are other types of dealerships, however, such as for appliances.

Starting Your Own Business

Experts who have studied the growth, success, and failure rates of new businesses agree on which steps are necessary for starting a business in order to have the greatest chance of surviving the crucial first years. A lot of careful thought and planning is required—most experts suggest at least a year of research into all aspects of the prospective business before making any com-

mitments. Preparing a business plan is an extremely important first step. The largest cause of business failure is getting all excited and jumping into things before the owner has done enough planning. The following 10 points should be thoroughly understood, planned, researched, and written out.

I. Is the Idea Workable?

Lots of very attractive ideas simply won't work. Sorry. I once worked in a natural grains bakery that made delicious breads. The bakery had an excellent location and had large sales—we couldn't make the bread fast enough for all our delighted customers and were usually sold out by 1:00 or 2:00 P.M. Within nine months, however, the owner had to declare bankruptcy. The problem? He had not accurately calculated what it cost to make and sell the bread and was selling it for less than it cost to produce. The more bread he sold, the more money he lost!

If you're thinking, "Nobody could be that stupid," you're wrong. Many people have made the mistake of thinking that because they have a very good product, they can make a good business selling it. This simply is not true unless the product is competitively priced. Most people will not spend $6

Meet Douglas Rodriguez

Chef and Restaurant Owner

Ever since he can remember, since he was a boy, Douglas Rodriguez has wanted to be a chef—never a fireman or a policeman or anything like that. His idol was Julia Child. "Watching her on TV was very entertaining for me," he says. "As soon as I was old enough to work, at the age of twelve or thirteen, I bought my first set of pots and pans and started a cookbook collection. I always knew what I wanted to do. I was very focused on what I wanted to do."

What Rodriguez finds most exciting about his job is that it's constantly changing. He can work with new ingredients, change his recipes, meet new people. "I enjoy what I do so much that I technically don't call it work," he says. "This is what I enjoy doing. I enjoy being here, coming to the restaurant." He also says that it's necessary to be aware of what other restaurants are doing, what the competition is doing, what other successful chefs are doing.

When he was asked how accessible the restaurant field is to Latinos, he says that it's big and becoming bigger. "Half the restaurant sous-chefs in New York are Hispanic. Sous-chefs are the second in command. They're either Mexican or from Puerto Rico, Argentina, Nicaragua—from somewhere in Latin America. I know a lot of the better chefs in the city. Sous-chefs will become chefs at restaurants—that's the natural progression. . . . Anything to do with Hispanics and food is a very big growing area."

According to Rodriguez, going to culinary school is a shortcut but not essential. Experience plays a much bigger part. "Like art school," he says, "out of one hundred graduates, three or four artists—the rest just know theory. Same with culinary school. Maybe a hundred kids go to it. Ten years later only two good chefs were in that class. Schooling is a way to get there a little faster, but it's not essential."

He thinks that being a chef and owning a restaurant go together, and that a very important qualification is business knowledge. Communications skills are what he considers his most important tool. He communicates to his staff how he wants things done, having sometimes as many as 10 meetings a day with other chefs, with the dishwashers, the waiters, bus people, and bartenders, constantly telling them what he expects—and complimenting them when they do it.

The starting salary in the field is $50,000 to $75,000 per year. Rodriguez works 60 to 65 hours a week, and he enjoys it. His organization is very big. "I have people that can do things," he says. "I'll write a recipe and give it to one of my chefs. I might cook two or three times a week and show somebody how to do something."

His advice to young people just beginning their business careers is to be sure it's something they enjoy doing. "I think that if you're going to be good at something, you should enjoy what it is. Most people that are successful really enjoy what they do, so it doesn't seem like work."

for a loaf of bread, which is what this owner would have had to charge to make even a small profit.

You will need to do extensive research to find out if your business idea is workable. If you are going to sell a product, how much will that product cost to produce? What competition will you have, and at what price are they selling their product? What is the potential market for the product? If you are going to sell a service, ask the same questions, substituting the word *product* with *service.*

Probably more businesses fail because the owners let their emotions run away with their good sense than for any other reason. They are so thrilled with the idea of owning their own business that they start up without sufficient research into whether their plan is practical.

II. The Business Plan

The thorough research you did for step one will be the foundation for your business plan. This plan should cover at least the first five years of your prospective business operation. Of course things won't go exactly as planned, but the fact that you have planned will make you that much more ready to deal with whatever comes up. And the fact that you have written down your plan will remind you of what needs to be done when the time comes to do it.

You don't have to reinvent the wheel, so don't panic. Hundreds of thousands of people have started businesses, and succeeded, before you. And a large number of them are willing and even eager to help. From the federal Small Business Administration to your local Hispanic Chamber of Commerce, there are many experts available to assist you in the planning stage (see Spotlight Stories on pages 18 and 22). These experts will be able to advise you about what types of business licenses you will need and how to apply for them. They will know how to figure overhead expenses for your business and what to economize on and what not to economize on. For example, a retail business needs a good location even if the rent is higher.

Among other things, your plan should include knowing the potential market for your goods or services, a description of your competition and how your business will differ, an estimate of the time needed to develop the business, the amount of money needed to launch the business and how you will get it, and a forecast of anticipated profits.

After writing your business plan, have it reviewed by a qualified professional and carefully consider the suggestions made.

III. The Type of Organization

The way you organize your business will be determined by many different factors, most of them economic—that is, the organization will be chosen on the basis of making the most profits and paying the least taxes. The good news is that the type of organization can be changed as the business grows or diversifies or needs more money or whatever changes occur.

A sole proprietorship is the simplest form of organization and requires the least amount of rules and paperwork. The sole proprietor is the boss, reporting to no one. He or she is also the only one responsible. There is no distinction between business and personal income or business and personal debts. Any income or loss is reported on the owner's personal income tax return. Usually small businesses start as sole proprietorships and may later incorporate to avoid personal liability.

When two or more people operate a business together, the type of organization is called a partnership. The partners share the profits or losses equally. A partnership files a separate business income tax return, but the profit or loss is reported on each partner's personal tax return. There can also be special types of partnerships, such as limited partnerships in which the limited partner invests money but does not participate in the running of the business. The written agreement between partners, whatever it is, is recorded with the clerk of court in the community in which the business is located.

A corporation is the most formal and complicated type of business organization. The owners are shareholders in the corporation, and the corporation exists as a separate individual. The "articles of incorporation" of a corporation have to be approved by the secretary of state in the state in which the business is located. The advantage of a corporation is that the shareholders' risk is limited to their original investment—they aren't responsible for the debts of the corporation. They are responsible for declaring any profits they receive on their personal income tax. This means that the profits are actually taxed twice: once for the corporation and once for the individual shareholders.

There is a special type of corporation, called an S corporation, which is more like a partnership except that it keeps the limited liability of a regular corporation and the profits are taxed only once. The number of shareholders in an S corporation is limited so that very large businesses are not eligible. This can be a very good type of organization for a business that two or more people are starting together.

IV. Choosing a Name

It's your business, you can call it whatever you want, right? Wrong. There are more rules and regulations, copyright laws, and trademark registrations than you might easily imagine. Particularly if you have hopes that your business might grow beyond your neighborhood, you need, again, to do a little research to be sure the name you choose hasn't already been chosen. Nothing could be more discouraging—and similar things have happened to a lot of people—than to build a thriving business selling Tia Maria's Tamales (your very own aunt and her very own recipes) and then to get a letter saying you're being sued by the Tia Maria's Tamales Corporation in Turkey Run, Nebraska, for trademark infringement.

Of course it is a good idea to include in the name a reference to the type of product or service you're providing. Even huge corporations like IBM started out with a descriptive name: International Business Machines. So

Would You Like to Own a Car Dealership?

According to Ernesto Ancira, the starting salary in the car dealership field is half a million to ten million dollars a year, depending on the size of the dealership. Needless to say, that kind of job is in demand. However, the minimum investment required is about $800,000 for smaller dealerships and up to $10 million for larger dealerships. After that you would need to have, or borrow, the money to buy your inventory from the manufacturer, and 500 cars cost a lot.

Ernesto's week, during which he would work 60 or more hours when he first started in 1971, is now more like 30 hours. This is because he has surrounded himself with good managers in his nine different car dealerships and three motor home dealerships. Basically he comes into his office, looks through his managers' reports to find out what's happening and what's not happening, goes through his mail, and that's it. About once a month he makes a television commercial.

Ernesto grew up in Mexico City, went to college at St. Edward's in Austin, Texas, and went back to Mexico City to work in marketing first for Gillette and then for Kimberly Clark paper products. Kimberly Clark was going to send him to São Paulo, Brazil, and he didn't want to go. On his way to Wisconsin to talk to them about it, he stopped in San Antonio. He found out that a car dealership had become available and the Mexican community was putting a lot of pressure on General Motors to select a Mexican to own it. Ancira had the good luck to be in the right place at the right time, and the good sense to realize it.

He says that he wasn't particularly attracted to cars. "It's one of those things that comes along as you live life and you have to jump on an opportunity and sometimes it may not be exactly what you had in mind. Or maybe you didn't have anything in mind, but you were open and flexible enough to capitalize on things that would come up as you went along."

When Ancira was asked how difficult this field was for Latinos, he said, "Well, I wouldn't say that for Latinos it's difficult. I think that for anybody it's difficult." He goes to high schools sometimes to talk to kids, especially Hispanic kids, and one question he's usually asked is that since he's Latino, how did he get to where he is? He responds, "The question is like saying that because I'm Hispanic I probably shouldn't be here. . . . I've got one advantage over you guys. I grew up in Mexico City where no one ever told me that I couldn't do it. I didn't know that, and that's the difference."

Ernesto Ancira thinks that programs that offer special assistance to minorities send a conflicting message: "If I need special help, then I believe I'm not as good. . . . The reason I'm here is because I thought I could do it. That's the first thing. For some reason, in this country we are led to believe that we can't do it. You've got to have the belief in yourself that you can do it. And when you start to believe you can do it, then you can do it."

after you've selected a good descriptive name like Tia Maria's Tamales, the first step, if you're planning on a business that will operate only locally, is to check the DBA (Doing Business As) register at the county clerk's office. If you have hopes that the business may expand to be statewide, the name should be cleared and recorded by the secretary of state in the state where you live. This is a necessary step if the business is ever to be incorporated.

You need to check with the state government to see if your business name must be registered. Sometimes banks need a notice from the state that the name is registered before they will let you open a business account in that name. But whether the business will be conducted only locally or not, you must avoid infringing on someone's registered trademark. This can only be determined by checking with the U.S. Patent Office, Trademark Registration.

All this may sound complicated, but in fact the searches for existing company names can be done quite easily and quickly on the Internet, which features both Yellow Pages (www.yellowpages.com) and White Pages (www.whitepages.com) of telephone directories, as well as trademark search services (www.uspto.gov).

V. Raising the money

Many promising businesses fail in the first two years because of insufficient capital. It is absolutely essential to raise enough money to see the new business through the very difficult first two years. Obviously the entrepreneur who can finance a new business from his or her own money is in the best position to profit from success because the profits don't need to be shared with partners or shareholders.

If you don't have enough of your own savings, there are a variety of funding sources such as state and federal funding programs, Small Business Administration programs through banks, SBA small business loans, and industrial development grants. Information about these sources of loans can be obtained from your local Hispanic Chamber of Commerce or the local office of the Small Business Administration (see Spotlight Story on page 18). The main thing to remember is that any loan will have to be paid back with interest, so the cash flow from the business will have to be enough to cover it. A debt load can be a real burden for a struggling business.

Another source of financing is other people's money. If you don't have your own money and you don't want to assume debts by borrowing, you can try to find investors to put up risk capital.

It's called risk capital because the investor is risking the money with the hope of sharing in future profits. It's like a gamble with the investor betting on the success of the company. The disadvantage of having outside investors is that they become co-owners of the company in exchange for risking their money.

Raising money is an area where Hispanics may have a strong advantage. Not only are there more loans available to minorities for starting businesses, but the larger and more tightly connected family relationships in the Latino culture may result in several family members' pooling their resources to get a business going.

VI. Holding Expenses Down

It doesn't take a mathematical genius to see that there's a very strong connection between the previous item and this one. The more you can keep expenses down, the less money you will need to raise.

Employees, with their salaries and payroll taxes, are a big expense. You can count on working hard for very long hours doing as much as you can yourself while getting your business started. Again, the Latino network of family and friends is likely to pitch in to help and may be your biggest asset. What you cannot do yourself or within your family can be contracted out—many small firms and individuals (stay clear of the big expensive outfits) offer accounting and tax services, for example, for far less than hiring an accountant would cost.

Except for retail businesses, which require a good location, you should hold down the cost of business location. Calcom International, which sold $32 million worth of computer components in 2000, operated out of the owner's father's garage for the first year. Many businesses can be started from a home office or basement. If you think you need a fancier address for customers to send their orders to, there are mailbox services that call their boxes "suites" so that they sound like exclusive office space in expensive commercial areas.

If you are starting a retail or service business that requires work space and selling space, get the best deal you possibly can. This means, again, doing the research, finding out the leasing price of comparable sites (don't even think about building or buying when you're starting up!), and bargaining hard not only for the rental cost but also for the

maintenance services, parking area, and other benefits the landlord will provide.

VII. Keeping the Books

You have to know where your business stands financially at any given time. This is absolutely essential. To do this you have to keep accurate financial records and make frequent financial statements. Remember the bakery owner who went bankrupt because he was selling bread for less than it cost to produce and sell? That would never have happened if he had been keeping accurate books—or at least it certainly wouldn't have taken nearly a year and forced him so deeply into debt that he couldn't recover.

That much said, the next important point is to keep the bookkeeping process simple and to face the necessity of it squarely and calmly and without anxiety. In the previous section about keeping expenses down, it was mentioned that the best solution might well be contracting your bookkeeping to a CPA (certified public accountant) or small accounting firm.

The most basic tool is the checkbook. Of course you will have an entirely separate checking account for your business and never, ever, get your personal account and your business

Hispanic Chamber of Commerce

The Hispanic population of the United States was 35 million by the year 2000—larger than the entire population of Canada and the fifth largest Latino population in the world, smaller only than those in Mexico, Spain, Colombia, and Argentina. This has a tremendous impact on the culture of the United States through purchasing power, creation of wealth through new businesses, and political power.

Hispanic Chambers of Commerce, on the national level, state level, and on the level of individual communities, are taking an active and positive leadership role in this economic and social growth. In Oxnard, California, a community in which 70 percent of the population is Hispanic, the activities of the Hispanic Chamber of Commerce (HCC) serve not only the Latino business community but the whole community, enriching it economically and culturally.

The HCC in Oxnard provides contact among the businesspeople in Ventura County. It holds monthly meetings featuring guest speakers, for example someone from the Small Business Administration or the mayor, who addresses the city from there. Various businesspeople come in and give presentations about their businesses and how they started. It's not all strictly business, it's anything that concerns the community—what's going on, what the prospects are for the city.

When asked why there is a Hispanic Chamber of Commerce in addition to the general Chamber of Commerce, Mary Ellison, a member of the HCC's board of directors, explained, "We are more personally involved with the Hispanic community. Some of our Hispanic population are immigrants—they're not always trusting of the Caucasian community because they haven't always gotten the help that they needed there. They just feel a little more secure knowing that they're dealing with businesses open to Hispanics. We have been wooed by the various banks for the Latino base of business."

Most of the banks in Ventura County belong to the Hispanic Chamber as well as to the general Chamber of Commerce. The HCC has about 200 members from all over the county. Members do not have to be Hispanic businesses. A member may be a business in which a certain number of the workers are Hispanic, for example. "Farmers, Allstate Insurance, you can't say that they're Hispanic. I don't know what their origins are, but their workers and a lot of their managers are Hispanic," Mary Ellison observes.

The HCC is personally involved with the community. It has a scholarship program and is involved with the schools—its 13-member board of directors includes a school principal and a superintendent of a high school district. It had a goal of awarding ten $500 scholarships in 2001. Latino students apply for the scholarships and are considered on the basis of their grade point averages, activities, and future plans.

The money goes to the college of the student's choice, to the college's financial department in the name of the student. The HCC has various fund-raisers throughout the year, such as a golf tournament and a casino night. All the activities and the organization of the HCC are provided by volunteers who serve both businesses that are interested in the Hispanic market and Hispanic businesses that are looking for ways to get to a larger market.

For more information on the U.S. Hispanic Chamber of Commerce, visit their Web site at www.ushcc.com.

account all scrambled up together. Except for very minor purchases made from petty cash (keep that separate, too), every expenditure should be made by writing a check and recording the nature of the expense in the check record. All deposits to the bank account should be recorded on a deposit slip with the source of the money noted.

A balance sheet is a listing of the assets and liabilities of a business. The assets are cash, inventory, money owed the company (accounts receivable), fixtures and equipment, etc. Liabilities are the money the company owes for accounts payable and debts. The difference between the assets and liabilities is the net worth, or book value, of the company. The balance sheet shows the financial strength of the company at any given time, but not its profitability.

Profitability is shown by the profit and loss statement, also called an earnings statement. This statement shows whether the company is making money or losing money at a given time. For a business selling a product, for instance, the sales revenue would be the total value of goods shipped and billed in the particular period. The cost of goods sold (COGS) would be the material or ingredients and the cost of labor to produce the products. (Don't forget your own labor! You're not working for free, you know.) The difference between the two is the gross profit. After that you subtract the expenses not directly related to producing the product, such as rent, utilities, insurance, etc. What is left is the profit—or loss, as the case may be.

Neither the balance sheet nor the profit and loss statement by itself will tell the whole financial story of the business. A rapidly growing business might have great profits but a weak balance sheet because of a lot of debt. On the other hand an older company that is dead in the water might have a balance sheet with lots of assets from equipment and no debts, but not be making much profit.

For a small start-up business, the owner can probably handle the bookkeeping tasks discussed above. They aren't complicated, but you do have to stay on top of them. Eventually, as the business grows and thrives—which it should if you are mindful of these 10 necessary steps—there will be other accounting tasks, and you probably will want a CPA, and perhaps eventually a company controller, to handle the books.

VIII. Cash, Credit, and Financial Controls

Oddly enough, one of the major reasons why businesses fail (and over half of new businesses do fail) is success. When a business is expanding, particularly in manufacturing or distribution, cash is rapidly used up. Money has to be spent on materials and labor well before products can be shipped and money collected. So a small business can get into trouble when it has lots of orders and can't fill them or can't collect the money.

Be very careful about offering credit terms to new customers. Don't be afraid to ask for advance payment or to ship products COD (cash on delivery). If you do have accounts with credit, don't let them get far overdue (45 days is a good cutoff point) before applying pressure to collect. If you keep an up-to-date accounts receivable listing arranged by age of the account, you can see the overdue accounts at a glance. And, obviously, don't ship new orders or provide services to clients who are behind in paying.

If your business is growing, you may need to employ more people. Be sure you are aware of all the expenses that a payroll involves. In addition to wages and insurance there are federal, state, and local taxes that need to be paid.

When the business is expanding rapidly, you may find that you need to borrow money from a bank or find investors. You don't want to wait until the last minute and be all in a frenzy when you need more money. Before the time arrives (just in case it does), be sure you know the people at the bank where you have your business account. Take the time to have a chat now and again and let them know how things are going, so when you need a bank loan, they know who you are.

If you need to find investors, plan carefully so that you can show good management practices. Don't be afraid to ask for advice at this point. Your local SCORE office (see Spotlight Story on page 22) will offer counseling services and advise you how to proceed. Don't try to impress investors with glowing descriptions of potential profits—they can't have confidence in a business that is not clearly explained.

Financial controls are just as important in small businesses as in large ones. Many many sad stories are told of employees, particularly if they feel underpaid, skimming off money or walking off with inventory items. One basic rule is to be sure that the person who writes the checks and keeps the checkbook is not the person who reconciles the bank statement. Another important point is to keep the number of people who can sign checks to a minimum—and require two signatures for any checks you don't write yourself. Also, set a limit on the amount for which checks can be written by anyone else. A copy of the invoice or voucher should accompany every check submitted for signature. And the invoices should be compared with the purchase orders.

IX. Marketing

Obviously, nothing happens in business until something is sold. And before you can sell anything, the customer has to know about it. It is very difficult to reach potential customers, let them know about the merits of your product or service, and convince them to buy yours instead of somebody else's,

SCORE

SCORE (Service Corps of Retired Executives) is a resource partner with the U.S. Small Business Administration that provides free information and counseling to business owners. SCORE's 11,500 retired and working business professionals volunteer their time and expertise to help business owners—over 300,000 of them in the year 2000—solve the problems they face starting their businesses.

With 389 office locations across the country, SCORE is available for personal counseling sessions with business owners. You can find the office nearest you by calling (800) 634-0245, or by logging on to their Web page at www.score.org. They even have online counseling. You can also send an e-mail to contact.score@sba.gov, telling them where you are located and they will respond with contact information.

Bob Bronson is a volunteer counselor at the SCORE office in Ventura, California. With a degree in electrical engineering and a graduate degree in behavioral science, Bob had 17 years of experience with Texas Instrument Company in Dallas, Texas, as the executive in charge of profit and loss statements, then he became vice president of a manufacturing company in California.

"When I counsel people," Bob says, "I need not only my own experience, but the mental capacity of looking at someone who wants to go into a business that I have no experience with and helping them develop the market research that they need, the business plan to put it together so they can proceed with it." He finds that there is a certain amount of frustration when people come in with ideas that are not workable. "You've got to tell them that they're wasting their time, or give them the homework to do so that they come to the conclusion themselves."

When the people who consult him do have a viable idea for a business, Bob provides them with the information they need about market research, understanding the competition, putting a business plan together, getting financing, and other aspects of getting started. One woman came in to talk to Mr. Bronson just as she was preparing to sign a lease for a shop for the flower arranging business she wanted to start. He gave her an assignment to contact similar businesses outside the area and ask them one question: "What does it take to get started?"

The woman came back a week later all excited. She had found out that it had taken over a year before the successful floral arrangers she had talked to began making money. She decided not to sign the lease for the shop but to remodel her garage for a work space to use until she could build up a clientele. She came back a year and a half later to bring Bob a little flower arrangement and report that she was then ready to lease a small shop—which would have been disastrous for her to do earlier. "That sort of thing really makes your time worthwhile," Bob says.

In addition to offering one-on-one counseling with experienced business professionals, the SCORE office in Ventura offers business seminars in collaboration with local community colleges. In spring 2001 there were six such seminars, including marketing, financial management, building a profitable business, buying and reselling, preparing a business plan, and a full day of free information on taxes and government regulations. If you want to score in business, SCORE is a great place to go for advice!

so one of your first priorities will be to get this information to your potential customers.

The very best kind of publicity, because it's the most believable and is free, is word of mouth. For a small neighborhood retail business or service, this may be all you need. More likely, however, in these days of huge malls and commercial centers, you will need ways to get the word out to a larger area than your own neighborhood.

Paid advertising is very expensive, so you want to explore every possible method that you don't have to pay for, or that you don't have to pay very much for. Trade magazines usually have a "new products" section where new businesses can be treated as news, and local newspapers also report on new businesses in their business sections. The trick to getting this kind of publicity is preparing announcements and presentations that will catch the interest of business editors.

Well-designed flyers that can be handed out or posted where lots of potential customers will see them can be an excellent marketing tool. If you can include a coupon for a special deal or bonus of some kind—maybe a small gift or price reduction for people with the coupons—you will have a built-in way to evaluate the effectiveness of your flyers.

Coupons can also be used in paid advertising, again because they provide a method of finding out which marketing methods are the most effective. Don't advertise in several different media at once or use different marketing tools at the same time. It is extremely important to find out what kind of return you are getting for your marketing dollar.

When you are planning to pay for advertising, think carefully about who will be the readers or audience of that media. If you are starting a party catering business, for example, you need to let the people who have their parties catered know about it. Placing a small ad in a concert program could be a good approach—but what kind of concert? Rap? Mariachi? Classical? Quite likely the audience for classical music would be more likely to include wealthy people who give catered parties. Never mind what type of concert you prefer, figure out which kind your potential customers might prefer.

X. Company Policies

Think about what you plan to do long before the time to do it arises, and write your policies down as part of your business plan. If you don't, if you wait until the heat of the moment, you will find that by default you are establishing policies that you certainly didn't want. Nearly every employer who ever lived has at some time been asked to advance or loan money to an employee. Are you going to advance money to a worker who asks? It's too late to decide when you are listening to a desperate appeal. Before you hire your first employee, you need to have a written list of policies, and before you make that list you will need to know the federal and state labor laws and workplace safety regulations.

Here are just a few of the things your policies will have to include:

- Business hours. When will the business be open? What are the regular working hours for employees?
- Pay and pay periods. Will employees be part-time or full-time? Will they be paid a salary or an hourly wage? If they work overtime, what will overtime pay be? What is the policy for pay increases and when will the reviews take place?

• Fringe benefits. Will employees get paid vacations or paid holidays? Will you offer an insurance plan? Will there be travel compensation?

• Use of company equipment. Who will drive the company vehicles and for what purposes? Will employees be reimbursed for use of their own vehicles, and at what rate? Will employees have access to a computer for their own purposes?

• Company image. Will there be a dress code? What impression do you wish to make on potential customers and clients?

A very important thing to remember about writing your business plan is that the things you don't decide and control for yourself will come up somehow or other anyway—and if you haven't made the decisions, you may not like the way things turn out.

Buying an Existing Business

After considering all the things that must be done to start a new business, you may decide that buying a business that is already up and running is a better approach to owning your own business. It may be. That will all depend on the circumstances—and finding out exactly what those circumstances are is what will improve your chances of success.

I. Evaluating Yourself

Just as you need to do when starting your own business, you need to do a lot of careful research and homework when you buy an existing business. You need to start with a very careful appraisal of what you have to work with. No, not regarding the business. Regarding yourself.

Just because a business is available and the price is right does not necessarily mean that you are the right person to own it. What are your strengths and weaknesses? What do you enjoy doing and what bores you? Do you like physical hard work or working with your mind?

You have to work very hard, and usually long hours, to make a success of any business, so it had better be something you enjoy doing. If you're a morning person, don't buy a retail business that has to stay open until 9:00 or 10:00 P.M., or a restaurant that stays open for the party crowd after dinner. If you're a night person, don't buy a morning shuttle service that starts at

Juan Vargas and the Story of Party Star Piñatas

Party Star Piñatas is not Juan Vargas's first business venture, nor is it his family's first venture. When Vargas came to California from Costa Rica in 1964, he went to California State University in Los Angeles and then to Pomona College. He worked for a while for Lockheed in the aerospace industry, and then he and his brother Carlos started a business making camper shells. They had a factory and two outlets in Los Angeles. His brother died in 2000, but Juan's nephew is still working on the camper shells.

In 1985 Juan's sister Aurora stopped in Los Angeles on her way to visit a daughter in New Zealand. Aurora brought with her the idea of making piñatas because they had an aunt in Panama City who was making them. Another of Juan's sisters got excited about the idea and the family started making piñatas. About a mile from where they were living, they found a place called Party World that was interested in selling the piñatas. From there they sold to the whole Party World system of about 35 stores.

Juan's brother Oscar, who has degrees in computer science and a master's in international marketing, saw the opportunity to make the business a little bigger. Oscar called the company Piñata Party, but they learned that a company in Florida already owned that name, so they changed it to Party Star. Oscar was busy with a big corporation selling motorcycles, so as the piñata company grew and more people got involved, Juan came in and started taking over the business because Oscar and their sister couldn't handle it all.

Although Party Star Piñatas is now nationwide—you can find them in any Wal-Mart store in Texas, for instance—they mainly do business in California, Utah, and Colorado. Juan's daughter Jessica is the office manager and CEO, and Juan is in charge of sales and deliveries. "Most employees are Latino," he says, "from Mexico, Guatemala, different areas, because they are the people who have the ability to make piñatas. They have that skill; their hands are so quick. They do things so well it's incredible. It seems to me that people from Latin America have that thing to make something very nice. Our piñatas are very nice—the average price is $13. We make dinosaurs, party stars, humanoids. The only thing we avoid are licensed characters. Just about anything you want, we make."

Juan Vargas is proud of his company, and he has every right to be. His piñatas are made, and made well, by adults making $7 per hour to start and up to $12 per hour with more experience. Another piñata maker might have a big factory in Rosarito or Ciudad Juárez and illegally use children to make piñatas for 2 or 3 pesos a day.

The work is hard and there is a lot of pressure from vendors who don't order far enough in advance, but Vargas gets a lot of satisfaction, too. "Sometimes I make deliveries on Saturdays," he says, "and bring a full truckload of different kinds of piñatas—maybe 500 to 600 different kinds to choose from. . . . I see the kids so happy, and the moms and dads. That's the rewarding thing for me. I know that every time we sell a piñata, there's going to be a lot of kids happy."

6:00 A.M. for early commuters. If you're painfully shy and don't like to meet new people, you don't want to cater parties. And so forth. So begin by making a careful and honest inventory of yourself and what you want, what you're good at, and what someone else will have to do for you.

II. Evaluating the Present Owner

Why is the business for sale? Is it really because the current owner wants to retire and move to Florida? Or does he know something you don't know? If you already know the seller—perhaps because you work for him or her or because the owner is a member of the family or a friend—you have a very big advantage. You know that your uncle wants to sell his business because your aunt insists on moving to Chicago where she can be near their grandchildren—and he's decided that after 30 years of marriage he might as well go with her. You know that your boss has high blood pressure and his doctor has told him he has to start taking it easy.

With strangers, you don't know, but you do need to find out. What you need to find out is basically how much you can trust them. Ask for references. Ask for permission to talk to the owner's business associates, banker, employees, and competitors. If there's nothing to hide, the seller will be glad to give you these references. If you sense danger signals here, back off. When you go on to the next step, which is evaluating the business, you need to be confident that what you see is what you get, and you have to be able to trust the seller.

After you've done a little nosing around and found out that the business owner is just what he seems to be—open, friendly, honest, and well-liked by his customers, business associates, and even competitors—should you go ahead with the deal? Wait a minute. How much of the success of the business depends on the relationships this person has developed, particularly with his customers? Are they going to go away when he goes away? This is something to consider.

The relationship between an owner and his business is complicated. Is the current owner willing to work with you for a while to ease you into the way he does things, introduce you to his suppliers and employees and customers,

and make the transition as smooth as possible? These arrangements should all be spelled out in writing as part of the sales contract.

III. Evaluating the Business

Get help. Unless you are already an established expert in the field, you really need unbiased assistance in evaluating the financial health of the business. And even if you think you are an expert, it never hurts to get another opinion. Here are just a few of the things that you may need to consider, and none of them is immediately apparent or even very easy to find out about.

In evaluating the assets of the business, you can't just accept the figures on the balance sheet. Is the inventory really salable? Or is it outdated? How about the equipment? Is the machinery used in manufacturing the product in good condition or does it need expensive repairs or even replacement? If the building is part of the deal, does it comply with local and federal codes? Remember that the present owner may be permitted to be in violation of regulations that were enacted after he already owned the business, but a new owner would not be. One unfortunate buyer learned after she purchased an aerobics studio that she was required by the city to construct 20 additional parking spaces. That unexpected expense nearly bankrupted her during her first year.

Working through a reputable business broker is usually worth the fees charged. It is the broker's business to be sure that the deal is reasonably good for both buyer and seller. If it isn't, then the broker won't be in business long. If you don't want to buy through a broker, you can still hire a consultant to advise you, or you can visit a SCORE counselor (see Spotlight Story on page 22), who will either advise you or find someone knowledgeable to do so.

IV. Determining the Sale Value

You have decided that the business is right for you, that the owner is on the up and up and will help you through the first month, and your research and investigations indicate that you can be successful with this operation. You want it. Now the big question is how much should you pay for it.

Sale price can be determined several ways. One way is to use a multiple of the book value (which is the net worth of the company as shown on the balance sheet when liabilities are sub-tracted from assets). This method of setting a price would apply to businesses such as retail stores with their inventories, manufacturing companies with extensive machinery, and transportation companies. If such a company is losing money, however, it may actually be worth less than the book value indicates. Be sure to have an outside accounting firm audit the books.

For service organizations a more accurate way of evaluating price would be the earnings record of the business as reflected in its profit and loss statement. A business that is growing very slowly, if at all, might sell for five or ten times the amount earned after taxes. On the other hand a rapidly growing business in a strong economy might be worth 25 or 30 times the yearly earnings, since the expectation would be that the earnings will continue to increase at the same rate.

V. Making a Business Plan

That's right. You will need to go through exactly the same steps that are required for starting your own business from scratch. The difference is that when you buy a business you have a lot more established facts and available information as you go through the planning stage. You have the previous owner's methods and procedures to evaluate as you decide upon your own. Some of them you may decide to keep as they are, at least for a while. Others you will see immediately need to be changed drastically. Either way you will need to do the research, think things through, and write your business plan out in detail.

Franchising

A franchise is a method of distributing products and services in the same way that the parent company, called a franchisor, does. This means that the person buying the franchise, called a franchisee, uses the same business system that the franchisor has developed. An example everyone is familiar with is McDonald's. Every McDonald's has the same menu and makes hamburgers the same way; each uses the same famous golden arches, decorations, promotions, and even napkins; but each McDonald's has a different owner.

There are over 3,000 franchisors, many of them very well known, such as McDonald's and Pizza Hut and Dunkin' Donuts, but hundreds and hundreds of others that are not so well known. The very big and popular franchises are very expensive to buy, particularly the famous fast-food franchises. Many of the smaller ones are more affordable.

The advantages and the disadvantages of buying a franchise are closely related. On the one hand you receive the benefits of the marketing, business methods, policies, and name recognition of a proven, successful business. (Although franchises can fail, of course, their failure rate is much lower than that of individual start-up businesses). On the other hand you pay a lot for the advantages, including the original franchise fee and a percentage of the profits of the business.

Before buying a franchise, you need to go through many of the same steps that you would go through in buying any business: evaluating your own strengths and weaknesses, preferences and lifestyle; evaluating the owner, in this case the franchisor; evaluating the franchise itself and its profit potential. Remember that the franchising company makes its money by selling franchises, so of course they sell hard. You will need to do research beyond listening to their sales pitch.

Probably the best research you can do is going around to the owners of existing franchises and asking hard questions. For example, the franchisor promises to train you in their business methods. Ask an owner to evaluate the training he or she received—did the company live up to its promises?

Owning a franchise can be a good way of getting started in business, if you need the security of established methods and can follow a lot of rules and regulations without too much difficulty. Keep in mind, however, that one very big reason people want to own their own business is to be their own boss. This will not be the case with most franchises. Franchises work because all of the franchises of a particular company are operated exactly the same way. And that won't be your way. But it will be a way to get good experience in business.

PART 2

Profiles of Success

Oscar Centeno

Owner of Oscar Centeno Trucking Company

Oscar Centeno owns and operates the Oscar Centeno Trucking Company, which has its headquarters in San Bernardino, California. "One of the things that I recall as a child in El Salvador," Oscar says, "is watching the trucks. I used to see these tankers, you know, the ones that carry fuel and things. And I used to look at them and say, 'When I grow up, I'm going to get one of those. At least the driving position. I'm going to drive one of those.'" Oscar kept his promise to himself. It took time, though, and a lot of hard work, before he got his first big rig.

Oscar was born in El Salvador on January 25, 1955, to teenage parents. His mother was 15 and his father 16, and their brief marriage was over before Oscar arrived. Both eventually married again and raised families. Oscar lived with his maternal grandmother and went to public schools in El Salvador through junior high school. When he was 14 years old, his mother left El Salvador to come to the United States. Two years later Oscar followed, but he lived with his father in California. His plan had been to continue his schooling, but that didn't work out.

"The conditions in which I was living, with my father, were just not right," he says. "There was no support for education. I just made the choice of starting to work right away, janitorial work with a big company, High Rise Building Maintenance."

Not only did he start working right away, but within a year of arriving in California, Oscar got married. His wife, Anna, was also from El Salvador. In 1973, when Oscar was 18 years old, their son Joshua was born. One of the janitorial jobs he worked on was at a Methodist church, where they offered Oscar the position of church custodian. "I was doing a little bit of janitorial work," Oscar remembers, "but was also handyman and caretaker of the place. That was good. I was about twenty years old. After that I was working for the church double shifts because my wife didn't work, and we were just trying to make it."

Oscar didn't speak English when he first moved from El Salvador. He had had an English class in junior high school, but he knew just a few words. Gradually he picked up English from reading and listening. "I think I naturally had a good ear. I did get a mail order course in English and I used to listen to the records," he says. "I had that course for some time . . . didn't finish it. I picked up some from there, and talking to people. Mainly just out on the street."

He worked as custodian at the church until the end of 1977. Even working double shifts, he found he wasn't making enough money. He had heard that truck drivers made good pay, so that gave him the motivation to try for a job driving. He couldn't get into that kind of work immediately because he had no experience, but he knew that a lot of truckers worked the docks, delivering and picking up freight. "So I went down on the docks and started knocking on doors looking for work," he says.

As luck would have it, the owner of Condor Freight Lines happened to be out on the docks that day. Oscar went up to him and asked if they needed any workers. "No, we don't need anybody," the owner said, "but I like your attitude. I don't see people nowadays doing this, particularly as young as you are. I can't give you a driving job, but I will give you a part-time dockworker position working four hours every night."

Before long that four hours turned out to be sixteen or eighteen hours a day. Oscar liked the work, and he was eager to make money. The first check he got from Condor Freight Lines was three times as much as he had made at the church. He knew that was the place for him, particularly when daughters Claudia and Michelle joined the family in 1978 and 1979.

From his job as dockworker, Oscar was promoted to different categories of the freight business, first as a dock supervisor. Then he began driving for Condor Freight, first as a city driver, which meant he was making pickups and deliveries in town. Later he did line driving, which was driving longer distances.

Before beginning to drive, Oscar had to pay a truck driving school, "which was a rip-off," he says, "because they didn't actually give me the training. Because the laws at the Department of Motor Vehicles at the time were very lenient with the exams and driving skills, it only took me two weeks to get my license. But I had to have proof that I had been to the school, and they took me to the DMV to take the test . . . but it was not like I came out of there knowing a lot about driving. . . . The sooner they give you the license, the sooner you have to pay them."

Oscar worked for Condor Freight Lines for four or five years. He worked rapidly into a management position, and the owners were very supportive. Unfortunately, the company began going through difficult times and had to cut back on their payroll. The controller at the time saw that Oscar was one of the employees making more money. "He thought that by getting rid of me they wouldn't have so much of an expense," Oscar says. "Cutting corners. And I was one of the corners."

After leaving Condor Freight Lines, Oscar drove for another company, but that one wasn't as financially sound as Condor had been and soon went out of business. By then Oscar knew a lot of people who said they would give him the freight if he had his own truck. "Just get your truck," they said, "and we'll give you the business to keep on going." It was the early 1980s, and he had saved enough money to put a down payment on his first rig.

"I was lucky," Oscar remembers. "I was very fortunate that customers gave me their business. I don't know if it was my sales, my hard work, the service, or the dedication I put into it, but people would always look for me." The fam-

ily was able to survive, pay their bills, pay for the truck and the fuel and insurance, and make a living. Another daughter, Monica, joined the family in 1983.

Oscar drove his first truck about two years before getting another one. And then another year came and another truck. Oscar liked the driving. He enjoyed getting to know different places, driving the California coast on Highway 101, seeing the beautiful scenery of the coast and the mountains. He also liked meeting different people, studying their attitudes, dealing with his employees and his customers.

"Part of it was like baby-sitting grown-ups," he says. "I seemed to be a father figure to my drivers and mechanics. I probably went too far with getting involved with their problems, letting them have advances on their earnings. It was a problem sometimes."

The slow steady growth continued until the early 1990s when Oscar began working with a large company that had lots of freight, and Oscar Centeno Trucking began to grow rapidly. Every year he would buy one or two more trucks, until he had a fleet of ten. His largest customer was providing him with half a million dollars' worth of business every year. But there were problems.

"The trucking business is so saturated that it's very competitive," Oscar says. "And this company, the one that was giving me the largest portion of my work . . . they would make me do things because they felt like they were giving me so much, and that I had no other choice but to do it. Sometimes they wouldn't pay for trips. They would expect me to move trailers from one place to another without payment. They didn't feel they had to pay."

By 1998 Oscar Centeno was in a difficult position. In addition to the problems he had with his biggest client—problems he felt were an expression of racism because the company had the attitude that a Hispanic-owned business would have to put up with extra work for no pay—he was also finding that he had no time for his family or his emotional and spiritual life. Like many owners of successful businesses that experience rapid growth, Oscar realized that all his time and energies were going into the business, with nothing left over for other aspects of life.

In 1989 the Centeno family had moved into a spacious house in Rialto, California, but Oscar wasn't home much to enjoy it. Like many, many other owners of successful businesses, Oscar felt isolated, as though he were a stranger in his own home. His children were used to looking to their mother for guidance and discipline and advice.

"I sometimes feel as though I don't exist," he says, "as though I'm not really there when I am there."

Oscar confronted his largest customer and let them know that he would no longer be able to provide the extra services for no pay that they had been expecting. The company took their business elsewhere, a loss of $500,000 per year for Oscar Centeno Trucking.

It seemed almost impossible to cut back on the family's expenses, however. By 2001 Oscar's son and two oldest daughters were all in college, and the youngest was about to graduate from high school. Like many Latino families, the Centenos place a very high value on giving their children the higher education they hadn't been able to have.

All of the Centeno children are still living at home. Joshua is a psychologist who works for the Child Welfare Department while studying for his master's degree. Claudia, the oldest girl, is studying to be a dietician at Cal State San Bernardino, while her sister

Michelle studies English at Cal State Polytechnic in Pomona and plans to become a teacher. Monica, the youngest, is definitely headed for college—she has been in a special program for advanced students ever since the fourth grade. "She's benefited from watching the older kids, seeing them go to college," Oscar says. "I'm betting she's the one who will go the farthest in an academic career."

Oscar's pride in his children is mixed with regret that he couldn't spend as much time with them as he wanted to while they were growing up. When Joshua was playing football for Glendale High School, Oscar went to the games whenever he could. But on many game nights he was on the road driving because a driver called in sick or a customer needed an emergency delivery. "My kids would tell me I was crazy for working so much," Oscar remembers, "and then say, 'Oh, by the way, Dad, I'll need a car when I start college.'"

Like most successful entrepreneurs, Oscar Centeno realizes that the costs of a business don't all show up on balance sheets and profit and loss statements with dollar signs in front of them. His business made a profit of slightly over $100,000 in 2000. He has enough equipment—eight trucks—to handle more business, and says, "I wouldn't say no" if he suddenly got more customers. However, with six drivers in addition to himself—and the necessity of driving double shifts when one of his drivers calls in sick—he is more interested in achieving a balance in his life than in selling hard to get more clients.

Gabriel Chavez

Founder and Owner of Technology Resource Center

Technology Resource Center (TRC) is an S corporation, which is a closely held corporation with fewer than 35 stockholders. Actually, it has two: founder Gabriel Chavez and his minority partner, Mark Serres. In 2000 this corporation did $5 million worth of business, of which about $300,000 was profit. TRC has 90 employees and provides two services.

The first service is systems integration, which means the company sells a communications system for transferring data from one point to another on radio frequencies. Instead of voice products they sell data products. For example, a water district might have a well 20 miles out from their central headquarters. They want to know if the well is pumping, how many gallons it's pumping, whether the tank is full, and so forth. Instead of having an employee drive back and forth to find out, they want the information to be sent over a radio frequency. TRC has the engineering skills to design the data transfer system the water district needs.

The other service is maintenance and repair for power plants and refineries. This service is for ongoing contracts, which provides stability for TRC. "I don't have to be selling over and over," Chavez says. "With those ongoing contracts comes the need to check in with them daily, find out where they're going and what their needs are. Based on that, then that sets up the day. We know what people we need, with what skills, at what location, at what cost, and for how long. It's as simple as that."

There probably aren't many people for whom the process would be "as simple as that," but Gabriel Chavez, who prefers to be called Gabe, is one of them. The two basic services that TRC provides exist because they are the areas of expertise of the two partners. According to Chavez, this is the most important thing about entrepreneurial companies: "Normally you lead from your strength. It would be hard for me to have started this business without some terrific amount of experience and education that leads me to this point. That's why we're successful at it, because of that past experience and education."

It was because he had no intention of letting his experience and education go to waste that he started TRC in 1996. His previous company, Nova, had failed, and he found out, to his shock, that in spite of his background and ability, employers didn't want to hire anyone who was over 50. "That was an eye-opener," he says, "because I thought, 'My god, I can do anything!' Except the age was a big factor. So what I could do was start another company. That was the easiest thing. On June 20 of '96 we closed up Nova, and four months later, November 6 of '96, I opened up TRC with $90,000 in borrowed cash."

Gabe Chavez was born in the town of Gomez Palacio in Durango, Mexico, on May 28, 1945. His father, who is also named Gabriel, was in the construction business and was taking correspondence courses with the University of the Americas to become a civil engineer. Their grandfather had died, so his father had to work to support his mother and three sisters, Gabe's aunts, in addition to his own family.

When Gabe was seven years old, his mother died, leaving his father with Gabe and two daughters. His father remarried and sent Gabe to Los Angeles to live with a childless aunt. "I spoke perfect first-grade Spanish when I went back," he says, "and everyone laughed at me. I had gotten through a couple of years of kindergarten school. I wish I had more." He learned English fast by necessity, through total immersion in school with only English-speaking teachers and students. He had to repeat first grade, but then he skipped second grade.

The aunt with whom he was living was a devout Catholic, so Gabe went to Catholic schools in East L.A.: St. Isabel grammar school and then Salesian High School. He graduated in 1963 from Salesian with a strong background in language skills and math. From there he went to Loyola University. He had a partial academic scholarship through the state, a Bank of America scholarship, and a scholarship from Western Gear for about $1,000. "Tuition was about $2,200 for an entire year," he remembers. "I got the rest of the help from my aunt and uncle who raised me. I was working. The first and second year of college I was working in a gas station. The third and fourth year I was working for a technical firm there in East L.A."

At that time, in the early 1960s, there were no scholarships specifically for minorities, but with a little help here and there and working part-time, Gabe was able to continue at Loyola. He loved sports, so he went out for basketball and made the freshman team. For the next year the varsity coach offered him a full scholarship, not as a player but as the team manager. He loved the sport and he enjoyed managing the team.

"I think the motivation came from my aunt, Maria Martinez, primarily," Gabe says about his determination to get an education. "My dad was still in Mexico and I visited him every summer. I saw that he was getting ahead. By then he had finished his correspondence school with the University of the Americas, and his business of building commercial and residential construction was getting bigger and bigger, so he obviously was economically successful. My aunt provided a moral center and unconditional love that made me believe I could attain my dreams. And you always want to be equal to, or, if you can, meet the expectations of your parents."

Gabe Chavez graduated from Loyola in 1968 with a degree in electrical engineering and went to work for Southern California Edison. At that time, nuclear power was just getting started. The first nuclear plant of any size was San Onofre I, near San Clemente, California. After he had a look at that plant,

Gabe decided to go back to graduate school and was offered a scholarship to the University of Cincinnati in Ohio. Just before he left, one of the managers at Edison offered him full pay to continue with the company while he was in school, because they wanted him back.

Gabe got a graduate degree in nuclear engineering from the University of Cincinnati in 1971. While he was there he met his future wife, Jana, who was studying at a nursing school nearby. They were married in 1972. Gabe found there was prejudice against minorities in the greater Cincinnati area and to a lesser degree in Jana's family, who were of German and Polish descent. "So that was interesting," he remembers, "getting over that. It was all marvelous. I don't think they knew how to spell *Mexican food* in Cincinnati in the '60s and '70s."

Back in California, Gabe's graduate degree qualified him for a management position at Edison. Pepperdine University was offering an in-house MBA program for managers at Edison, so he took that for a year and a half and completed all the course work in 1975. The big nuclear units, San Onofre II and III, were built, and Gabe was a key part of that process. During his years working for Edison, he and Jana had two boys, Tony, born in 1973, and Nick, born in 1976.

In 1982 Gabe decided to leave Edison because he didn't agree with their policies.

Because of his experience at Edison, hiring people and recruiting from companies across the country, Gabe Chavez knew many in the power industry. He joined Nova Power in the same year, 1982, as a top executive with stock options. He opened up a region for them in southern Indiana where there was a nuclear plant being built called Marble Hill.

"Those were some good times there, in '82 and '83," Gabe remembers. "But little by little, at the end of about a year with the contract, which was going very well, the utility we were working for ran into a huge cash flow problem and could not finance the construction of the nuclear plant anymore, so they shut it down. That was when Nova started to have problems."

Because of the difficulties at Nova, many of the minority partners wanted out, so Gabe started buying stock in Nova. He had faith that the company could find other work. "I set up shop in the basement of our Indiana home and started selling all across the coun-

try, all the way from New England to Texas to Florida, Kansas to Oregon. When I left Edison I wanted either more time or more money, so at least I got more money."

Gabe bought out all the other partners except the majority partner, so it was just the two of them owning and operating Nova. They ended up with contracts all over the country—he went to Texas for several months in '84 and '85 to run a job there, and then in '85 the majority partner asked Gabe to come to California to take over the whole business. This is what he did until Nova ran into trouble in 1996. "Nova went belly up," he says, "but didn't go bankrupt. We managed to pay off all our debts and financial liability and go away. Honorable, but still difficult."

Gabe had learned a lot at Edison and with Nova, far too much to waste just because he was 51 years old. That was when he decided to begin another business—and this time he would be the majority partner so that he could apply what he had learned. One problem Nova had had was that they bid for fixed-price contracts. If the bid ended up being too low, Nova lost money. The new business, Technology Resource Center, issued continuing contracts for maintenance and repair. "Another policy that I made here," Gabe says, "contrary to the other company, is to have very little home office overhead. Including our controller and officers, we only have three permanent members of staff on overhead [son Tony, partner Mark, and Gabe]. Everyone else is either on projects and working and billable or they're on the bench waiting for some work to develop. And again, that's to minimize expenses and maximize our survival capabilities."

TRC frequently uses subcontractors to lessen their financial liability on contract work, which is why they have a full-time financial person. This is Gabe's son Tony, who joined the company in 1998. In addition to being small, the home office operation is personal. They all answer the telephone because Gabe hates voice mail and wants to give his clients the personal touch. The office is reachable by Internet, fax, or answering machine after business hours 24 hours a day. That allows Gabe's end of the business to recruit and staff 90 positions. His partner's many clients, ranging all the way from Alaska to Mexico, can call in any time for assistance with any problems they're having.

After Gabe opened TRC in November 1996, with a minority partner who was able to provide the financing, the company did about $1 million worth of business in the first year, $3 million in the second year, and $5 million in the third year. The energy crises in California in 2000, which Gabe initially was afraid would bring a loss for TRC, turned out to benefit the company. "More than ever, independent power producers are just having to repair and maintain what they've got," he says, "and even build new ones. I expect that for the next ten years we'll be building power plants in California."

When asked what advice he had for young entrepreneurs, Gabe Chavez emphasized that education is the basis for everything. The other thing needed is experience. "I'm not so sure you can leap immediately from an educational base to a business without going through a good amount of experience," he says. "Mine happened to be that I worked for two or three large firms . . . so I had fourteen, fifteen years of large company exposure before I started going out. And then I also had the training of another entrepreneur, the Nova Power majority owner, Tom Teichmann. After that it started to become easy."

Abraham and Ana Corina Garcia

Owners, Calcom Computers

Abraham Garcia and his wife Ana Corina Garcia are in the business of selling computers. Lots of computers. They are primarily exporters from the United States to Mexico, where they establish warehouses and find resellers. The resellers may be consultants, or they may be retail stores. Calcom's customers have their own businesses and need to find products at a good price. The Garcias are a volume source for their customers, with total sales of $32 million in 2000.

Abraham buys marked-down components—for instance, one or two thousand monitors, two thousand hard drives—and then offers the components for sale. In the computer industry, there are the major manufacturers—such as Apple and IBM, Compaq, Hewlett Packard—and these companies control a very large part of the market. There are also smaller companies that make computer components. When these smaller manufacturers overestimate their sales and wind up with extra inventory, they try to find another channel to move the excess products. Abraham is one of the buyers shopping for reduced prices on large volumes of components.

Calcom has 135 employees, 25 in the United States and 110 in Mexico. There are different departments in the Calcom Company: sales, warehousing, technical support, accounting, and administration. Calcom also has a shipping department with 10 trucks and traffic people who move the product. In Mexico the company has five warehouses, in Tijuana, Hermosillo, Culiacán, Tepic, and Guadalajara. In the United States there is one large warehouse in San Diego, where they receive the products, prepare the documents for export, and make the shipments.

Both Abraham and Ana Corina come from families of entrepreneurs doing business on both sides of the border. Abraham's father has an auto parts business in Tijuana and in the United States. Corina's father has a tuxedo rental business that buys tuxedos in the United States and exports them to Tijuana for rental. "So for us it was easy to decide to start a business," Abraham says. "It was what we knew when we were growing up." The two grew up in Tijuana, went to public schools, and met when they were in high school. Ana Corina has one brother and three sisters. Abraham came from a much larger family of nine brothers and two sisters.

Abraham's paternal grandfather was born in Zacatecas, Mexico. He and his wife came to the United States in the 1930s as fieldworkers in the Palm Springs area. The family was deported later, but not before Abraham's father and two of his brothers had been born in the United States and were therefore U.S. citizens. Then, in the 1970s, there was a "citizen abroad" law that stated that because Abraham's father was a U.S. citizen, all his children were, too. Abraham now holds a dual citizenship for the U.S. and Mexico.

Abraham's father lives in California now, but for many years he worked in the United States and lived in Tijuana. He started the auto parts business for his sons. "My brothers and I were always in charge of the business in Mexico," Abraham remembers. "In order to sustain the family, my father worked in the construction business as a laborer in the U.S."

After graduating from high school, Abraham went to the Insituto Technologico in Tijuana. He received his degree, the equivalent of a bachelor's in engineering, in 1986. At the same time, Corina was studying computer science at the same school. They married in 1986, the year that Abraham graduated. Ana Corina graduated in 1987.

For two years Abraham worked as an electrical engineer for the Motorola Corporation in Tijuana. He was a process engineer, which means his job was to make improvements on the production lines and to control production. If Motorola had a lot of rejected parts, Abraham had to figure out why and what to do to improve the situation. At the same time, Corina was working for a company in the United States called Nimax. This computer company had the idea to establish a warehouse for their product in Mexico. Corina was the sales manager selling to the Mexican market.

Early in 1988 Corina's boss at Nimax offered Abraham a job working in the purchasing department, for much better pay than he was getting at Motorola. Abraham took the job, and he and Corina worked together at Nimax for about six months. Unfortunately, the company was owned by two partners who were having serious disagreements. They decided that the only way to settle their differences was to go out of business. The value of the business was about $100,000; the Garcias couldn't buy it because they didn't have that kind of money. Suddenly they had no jobs.

"I thought of returning to the auto parts business," Abraham says, "but Corina didn't like [that idea] because she felt that I would always be under the control of my father and it wouldn't be good for her. I was happy with that, but she wasn't. So we didn't have any options but the computer business, which is what we had been doing."

During the two years since graduating, while they both had been working, they had saved money. Abraham had been working part-time with his father while working for Motorola, and they had saved about $35,000. To get started, they used one of Abraham's father's little places that had an office, and the garage of his father's house in Chula Vista, a suburb of San Diego. "So that was it," Abraham remembers. "I was doing the purchasing for the new business, and Corina was doing the sales. That was the first division that we had of the tasks of the business. We had no operation costs except our salaries, which were very low."

Abraham's and Corina's fathers did not help them financially, except by letting them use a small amount of office space, but the assistance they received from their families was far more valuable than money. It was the business sense that their fathers had gained through experience. The most important advice they got was to keep expenses as low as possible. Unlike other business owners, who frequently get into serious trouble by renting fancy office space furnished with impressive equipment, Abraham and Ana began with scarcely more than a telephone and an order pad. "The business made a profit from the beginning," Abraham says. "With the background that we had, we tried to reduce the costs. That was always the advice we had from our fathers. . . . They always wanted us to do something for ourselves. When you ask for help from them, they always think twice because they know [you'll] ask for more each time."

Another benefit they received from their fathers was an existing reputation in Mexico. "Some of our customers had known my father, and also Corina's father," Abraham says. "So we asked for prepayment, sometimes 50 percent, sometimes a little bit more, and then we put in the rest. And we had maybe

20 percent profit. We were starting to sell to resellers. Sometimes they ordered just one component from us. If I had a good deal on a hard drive, they would order just that. The other components they would buy through other people. Some of the customers bought only some of the components from us. Others bought them all."

In the beginning years of the business, Abraham and Corina, together and separately, had to cross the border two or three times a day. The Tijuana border crossing is the busiest international border in the world, with motorists waiting in lines for 30 minutes to an hour for each crossing. This slowed them down, but it certainly gave them time for planning policies. Years later they were able to get a border pass so that they could drive right through without waiting.

As the business grew, the Garcias tried to think through each step, to formulate policies in advance, to be working smart as well as working hard. Even so they have had some problems, particularly with employees. "We had some people who took some money from the accounts," Abraham says. "One of them was $100,000 back in 1994–5. One of my sources of pride was the controls that we have in the office—I always tried to establish controls for money and inventory. We always came up with new ideas to see that money from customers went directly to the bank so that our finances were in good shape, that we were responsible."

According to Abraham the largest problem occurred because of an employee that they trusted, and because of that trust gave a lot of responsibility. "What happens is that you have someone who you don't want to lose, so you start not wanting to put controls on them. That happened to me. We didn't control this person very strictly. We gave him flexibility and we didn't check. He was forging my signature. We wrote about 300 to 400 checks a month, and when we received them from the bank, I didn't go through them one by one. So there were one or two checks he put through every month, and by ten months later it came up to $100,000."

The employee who stole the money was put in jail, and the company has recovered some of the loss. Although Abraham's pride was punctured when he realized that he hadn't exercised enough control to keep the theft from happening, the situation showed the Garcias what changes they needed to make. They established that the checks from the bank were to be received at a separate post office box, and Abraham now looks at every check.

"I might not catch every one," he says, "but it won't be ten months later." They estimate their losses on inventory, which are less than half a percent because they do daily inventories of the expensive components.

Abraham and Ana are projecting to expand to nine warehouses in the next two years. The important factor to consider is the transportation that allows them to distribute their products. "We think of a route that will help us distribute," Abraham says. "Like we went to Hermosillo, and then to Culiacán, which is on the Pacific. It might cost $1,000 to put the product in Hermosillo, but only $200 more for Culiacan. We have trucks that unload in Hermosillo and then go on. So we're looking for that kind of route on the eastern side."

In addition to building a very successful business together, Abraham and Ana Corina have a growing family. They have four sons: Abraham Jr., born in 1989; Nahum, born in 1994; Yoab, born in 1996; and Isai, born in 1999. The boys were all born in Tijuana but are U.S. citizens because of the citizen abroad law. The Garcia family now lives in the United States, in Chula Vista, California, where their new home was completed in October 1998. "In Mexico we feel we need to learn a lot of things from the U.S.," Abraham says. "The first thing is how can we enjoy life more. Most companies go to Tijuana for the cheap labor. I grew up thinking of being in the U.S. as being always in Disneyland. Even though I am a citizen, I wanted to feel that it is my land. And that was the main reason why we moved here. I want my kids to have the best of two worlds."

The difficult task of balancing the demands of a growing business with the other aspects of their lives is something that Abraham and Corina have been very successful with. This is partly because they are business partners as well as marriage partners, and each of them brings very specific abilities to their business. It is also because they enjoy each other, their children, and doing things together. They like to travel and journeyed to Egypt in 2000 and to Greece in 2001. Their partnership is what made these trips possible.

Leticia Herrera

Owner and President of ECI Company

There are a lot of different ways to start a business. Leticia Herrera started hers by accident. In the early 1980s, in Chicago, Leticia was 22 and working for the county assessor's office. It was an election year, and part of her duties included organizing events for Hispanic voters. In the process she called a friend who worked for the Chicago Public School System to contact Hispanic teachers. As things frequently go in politics, her friend said that he would do her the favor if she would help him out by finding him a minority-owned janitorial service for a contract the school district needed to fill.

Leticia provided the names of a few Hispanic janitorial services; one of them signed a contract with the schools; the teachers showed up at the political rally. Everything was fine. At least everything was fine until two weeks before the contract was to be completed. Leticia got a call from the janitorial service saying they wouldn't be able to do the work because the job wasn't big enough. And Leticia wasn't able to find another service to do the job.

If there's one thing that Leticia lives by, it's keeping her word. The school district had delivered the teachers, and she was determined to deliver the cleaning service, even if it meant doing it herself, which is exactly what happened. She enlisted the help of her mother and her aunt, got brooms and mops and detergent and scouring pads and a bucket, bought insurance, and incorporated a business under the name Extra Clean, all in two weeks. The paperwork on the contract had all been completed, so all they had to do was change a few details.

The job turned out to be cleaning all the men's stalls at the huge school district central offices. When the two-day weekend was finished, the rest rooms were clean, and the school district was pleased with the work. "I paid my mom and my aunt," Leticia remembers, "and when I was doing the tally afterwards I found out that my big mouth only cost me $450 with the incorporating and everything, so I was happy. I thought, thank god, I kept my word and I'm done."

When she came home from work about two months later, her dad handed her an envelope, saying, "This has been here. What is it?" She had forgotten the name she'd made up for the company: Extra Clean.

"I thought, oh my god, another bill," she says. "I opened it up and it was a check for the work. I hadn't even priced it, because they had priced it. I looked at what the check was, I looked at what I had spent, and I realized I'd made as much in two days as I did in two weeks working at my job. The rest is history."

Leticia's personal history began in Chicago in 1960. Her parents, Maria and José Roberto Herrera, came from Durango to settle in Chicago in 1955. José had come illegally when he was 12 years old. Later he returned to Mexico and got married. He worked for the railroad, and Chicago was the end of the railroad line from Durango. In the 1950s it was usual for only the men to come to the United States while their families remained in Mexico. But Leticia's mother didn't agree with that custom.

"I married you to be with you," Maria Herrera told her husband, "not to be away from you. So either I go or we get a divorce." That was not usual for a Mexican woman.

"I guess you're coming with me," her husband said. Now both parents are U.S. citizens.

Maria Herrera, who was educated in Mexico, taught Leticia and her brother and two sisters how to read and write in Spanish, their first language, before they began school. The four went to Catholic schools, where Leticia says she learned how to sell: "You know they give you those quotas," she remembers, "and if you don't make your quota selling cookies or candy or whatever, tuition goes up. So what I did, I used to sell mine, and I sold all the stuff for my brother and sisters so that my parents—I saw them working so hard—wouldn't have to come up with the extra tuition. They gave you a $200 or $400 credit if you sold a lot, and I always exceeded the amount."

During her freshman year in high school, Leticia went to Mexico. Like many immigrants, Leticia's father would talk about going back to Mexico. "He never lived here, he never lived there," she says. "It's a big trade with many ethnic groups. They keep saying they're going back, so they don't live right here. But they never go back." Leticia told her father that she was going back to Durango for one year, and if he didn't bring the rest of the family within a year, she would come back but would never go to Mexico to live again.

In Durango Leticia went to a private school, a *colegio,* where the children of diplomats and dignitaries went to school, and studied in both English and Spanish. Her father visited her and realized that he was not going to move back to Mexico. He came back to Chicago, became a U.S. citizen, and moved to the suburbs. When her year in Mexico was up, Leticia returned to Chicago and went to an all-girls school for two years, then finished her senior year at a public high school, graduating in 1977.

She went to a two-year college, Triton, for an associate's degree in business administration, and was finishing her bachelor's degree at DePaul. In the meantime she had been working full-time, first at a medical company and later at the assessor's office. This was the position she'd been in when she took the fateful step of starting Extra Clean, Inc. on weekends. The first year they just got repeat business from the Chicago schools. By the second year Leticia had to make a decision: either continue in school to learn how to run a business, or actually continue running one. She dropped the school. By the

third year she had to quit the job at the assessor's office, too.

"I started growing and growing," she says, "but I was becoming an employment agency, not a profit company. And there was a lot of competition. But it wasn't just money. By the fourth year I could have quit and gotten a job and made triple what I was making from the business. So being an entrepreneur isn't just about money. What is a driving force is the independence of creating our own company. That we have no limits. And if I walk in with pink hair, or I walk in with an accent, it doesn't matter because I'm running it, and I make the decisions."

In 1995 Extra Clean, Inc. nearly went bankrupt because of the nature of the industry. The huge janitorial businesses were buying and selling each other, and the smaller operations were being squeezed out. "My business was my life in many ways. I was connected to it," Leticia remembers. "It was my child and I could not let it go until it almost died and I had to cut it off. But when I finally faced the fact that, okay, the business is going to go down—you don't want to recognize it, so you keep turning, turning the wheels, doing this, doing that, until one day it just falls." At that point Leticia realized that she had to let go of the close personal connection she had with her business if she was going to survive. She had been working hard. Now she had to start working smart as well.

Her attorney was telling her that she should close the business, and that if she did she would come out ahead. "Close the business today," he said, "and you keep $60,000, you keep this, you keep that."

Leticia said, "Wait a minute. You want to get paid?" When the lawyer said that he did, she told him that the day she closed her business would be the day she had no car, not one piece of jewelry, not a watch, and no money in the bank. "A lot of people trusted me," she said, "and that's why I have a business. I'm not going to have anyone else pay for that."

Her clients had been telling her, "You guys are good at everything else, but our areas of impressions are really bad." Leticia thought she could do something about it, so her company found their specialty niche, doing stone and marble. She let go of all the janitorial accounts and progressed to doing other structural cleaning and maintenance and specialty jobs. She even changed the name of her corporation— it's still ECI, but instead of Extra Clean,

Inc., the letters now stand for Excellence, Creativity, and Integrity.

Instead of trying to do everything herself, Leticia now has different managers and division supervisors, with a division for marble, a division for construction, and a division for specialty cleaning. "For example," she says, "since we came from the cleaning field, I may do the cleaning of the chandeliers at the Hilton. That's a $30,000 or $40,000 job, and that's a specialty. It's not your typical janitorial. So we do construction restoration and specialty cleaning. That's why our logo says, 'There's an art to what we do.'"

Leticia now makes a distinction between being the owner of the company and being the president of the company. "Many entrepreneurs have lost their businesses when they've grown to a certain level," she says, "because they're not good presidents. They're good owners. When they get to a level when things have to be delegated beyond themselves, they lose it. I now make two checks, as a president, and as an owner. I did that because it works for me. . . . I look at what I do as an owner and as a president. For example, suppose there's an error of $100. As an owner it doesn't make that much difference. It's only $100. But as a president, it matters. Why did it happen? How did it happen? How can we stop it? Many owners are not good managers of the business."

Because her experience has enabled her to see clearly the distinctions between an entrepreneur (the person who starts new ventures), the owner, and the person who runs the business, Leticia Herrera is now able to make more intelligent decisions. For her, success is not measured by dollars, although she makes well over $100,000 per year, but by being able to balance her work and her life—the quality of her life.

"I now know that I have an entrepreneurial spirit in me," she says, "so you know what I've done so that I don't put my business out of business? I've disconnected from my business—my business is my bread and butter, it pays the bills—and have gone into other ventures. Because I need that drive, I need that motivation, that risk, that adrenaline. Knowing and trusting yourself and what works for you is your best asset."

To satisfy her entrepreneurial spirit, Leticia now does joint ventures. She has gone into areas such as construction, ECI with other companies so that they each bring their own areas of expertise to the projects. In 2001 she was working on her fourth project as a joint venture with a window installation company. She manages the construction and they install the windows. "I don't make one hundred percent profit," she says. "Now I make fifty percent profit. But I'm getting their experience under my belt, and they're getting my experience under their belt. And we're both putting up resources. If we fail, we fail fifty percent. If we gain, we gain fifty percent, with less effort and a partnership relationship. Two heads are better than one!"

She was also exploring the possibility of a $12 million construction project for the federal government. As a minority and a woman owning her business, she brings minority participation to any project. "It would take me alone another five years to get to a twelve-million-dollar project," she says, "but in a joint venture I'm at the door now. We were put together by the Small Business Administration because they're looking for partnerships and joint ventures. There's a lot of criticism of federal agencies and government, but I am a product of their success, and so is Apple Computers, and so is UPS. I don't care what anybody says, it works, yet you must take action and never, never give up!"

John Leaños

Cultural Worker, Artist

"On my business cards I call myself a cultural worker," John Leaños says, "and there are several reasons for that. . . . I realize that *artist,* which I am, doesn't fully embrace the entire spectrum of what I do. I see myself as an educator—I am an educator. I'm a writer, a visual artist, a curator, a cultural critic, and a community organizer and activist. All these things that I do fall under this umbrella term of *cultural worker.*"

John's job description is abstract because art is always changing, and the artist must constantly redefine his work and its relationship to the community. "There aren't too many artists who work in studios and produce work and bring it into a gallery and sell it. Very few artists are like that. Most of us have the responsibility of creating interpretations for our work. Writing about our work. Being able to talk about our work in various different contexts. Being able to write grants. Being able to socialize and talk to different people and be community leaders in a sense."

One way to see the range of activities that artist John Leaños is involved in is to take the items in his "cultural worker" job description one by one. As an educator, John is teaching in a public high school in San Francisco called The School of the Arts. It's a magnet school for the arts, and John teaches a class titled Community Building. The idea of the class is to get the high school students involved in creative work outside the school, with nonprofit organizations, with artists, with people doing creative things. He teaches the class at 8:00 A.M. three times a week.

As a writer John is involved in a number of projects, including grant writing. He is also part of a group of three artists called "Los Cybrids" (their Web page is at www.cybrids.com), who have gotten funding to do a series of projects looking at computer technology and the Internet. They have created a series of events that they call performalogues, which examine the social, cultural, and environmental effects of the digital revolution. "That's introducing me into the world of performance, which I really haven't done before," John says. "I'm learning a lot about performance as well as writing and collaborating on ideas."

As a visual artist, John Leaños is involved in the creation of digital murals. "I think that digital murals are on the cutting edge," he says. "They are computer generated, meaning that they are done on a computer and the disk is brought to a billboard printing company and they print it up. It is printed up just like any other advertising billboard." He is curating a digital mural program at the Galería de la Raza in San Francisco. Curating is designing an art project and seeing it through to completion. His responsibilities are to write a curatorial statement explaining the purpose of the project, to find the artists and to look at their slides, and to select the work that will be displayed.

John Leaños was born into a biracial family, Mexican and Italian, in Pomona, California, in 1969. His father, also named John Leaños, had come to the United States from Guadalajara when he was seven or eight years old. The family lived in New Mexico briefly, then moved to Los Angeles. This was during the 1950s, when Mexicans were punished for speaking Spanish in school. At that time also, John says, "There was always this question, 'Are you Spanish or are you Mexican? What is your ancestry?'

So there's this really weird politics of identity that has racist undertones."

John's father delineated himself as having Spanish ancestry and tried to assimilate. He married an Italian American woman, Marie Eifani, John's mother. Marie's father was an immigrant from Tuscany, Italy, who settled in Chicago for a while and then brought his family to Los Angeles. That's where John's father and mother met and married and raised their children, three boys and a girl. John says that there was always racial tension between the two families.

"My *nona,* my Italian grandmother—when I was about three, running around as a little kid—she didn't like me," John remembers, "because I had a round face and I looked Mexican, she said. She eventually came around, but that was the story, because she didn't want us to be Mexican. My grandfather, who died when I was about four, did not approve at all of my father's side of the family. And also, when I was about six or seven, I was over in East L.A. with my great-grandmother and she said in Spanish about me, 'He looks so white. Why is he so white?'"

As a result of the racial tension, the two families more or less ignored each other. John's mother didn't want the children speaking Spanish in the house. John would often work with his father in construction, doing flooring jobs, and they would speak Spanish, so John picked up some of the language that way. "So I'm mixed race and I call myself 'mixtupo,'" John says.

John went to St. Joseph's Catholic School in Pomona until the eighth grade, then to Servites, a private all-boys high school. He graduated in 1986 and attended Mount San Antonio Community College for a year. After that, he moved to San Francisco and enrolled in San Francisco State University. "It was good to get away," he says, "but a lot of culture shock."

As an undergraduate at San Francisco State, he was studying humanities and doing a lot of reading and writing. "During that process I bought a camera and set up a darkroom in my closet," John remembers. "And just began to take pictures and pictures and pictures, and started to look at that. It was for me an artistic process. . . . I'd always been interested in art work, but living in Pomona, living in Los Angeles, you really don't get too much exposure to diverse expressions of art. At least I didn't. There wasn't really anything that clicked until I was up here. .

. . So I picked up my camera and shot a lot of photographs."

After John Leaños graduated from San Francisco State with a bachelor's degree in 1992, he went to Spain for a year and a half. He found that in the European culture the artist is respected more than in the United States. "I took up painting while I was there," he says, "and experimented, and spent hours late at night painting, and realized that I wasn't a good painter, but kept on doing it anyway."

While he was in Spain, John met the woman who would become his wife. Aurora, who is Spanish, worked in an office in Madrid. They met through a mutual friend and found they enjoyed each other's company. When John returned to the United States, Aurora came to visit him and they decided they wanted to stay together. They married in 1995.

In the United States, John worked for a year or so and then in 1997 enrolled in a three-year master of fine arts photography program. He found that one of the most valuable parts of his training in the MFA program was volunteering in middle schools and working with young people, doing murals with kids. The time that he was able to donate to schools and community organizations got him interested in how schools and communities work. He wanted to understand the issues and the complexities, to see how art can be meaningful to a community and define it.

"What I didn't want to do," John says, "was become involved in the 'art world.' Gallery shows and openings and chitchat and all that. I really wanted to be involved in the community and teaching. My interests were a lot broader than just creating an image. I'm interested in image making. I'm interested in the formal qualities of making an image, but I'm much more interested in how communities form, how people work together. . . . What the artist's responsibility is inside the community. So that's when I explored that here and started to get involved in the Galería de la Raza and do public artwork."

The Mission District in San Francisco is a rich landscape of mural painting from the Mexican tradition. The great Mexican muralists, such as Diego Rivera and Orozco, whose work was very literally revolutionary, inspired a political movement in the early 1980s when Hispanic artists in the Mission District painted murals in protest of U.S. occupation in El Salvador and Nicaragua. Twenty-Fourth Street in particular has been flooded with murals with many different themes.

"We were using this idea of muralism to keep in the tradition of the San Francisco Latino/Chicano mural in the city," John says, "but also moving it into this idea of computer-generated murals because a lot of urban Latino artists are using computers. There are a lot of photographers out there. We can say that the Galería has been painting on the Twenty-Fourth Street and Bryant mural for forty years. It's always been a rotating mural place. And only in 1999 were we able to get funding to put billboards up, which is the digital mural program."

Funding for the program came from various places, such as the Creative Work Fund, which is a local foundation. The Galería did the grant writing for a part of the program, and John and the group of artists he works with, Los Cybrids, did the other part. The job description in the grants is to find artists to hang the mural. The curator, John Leaños, basically chooses the artists and the artwork and designs a concept around what the themes will be. "I talk with them about the issues of a digital mural as a public artwork," John says. "It's very different from an artwork in a gallery."

Los Cybrids also won another grant from the Creative Work Fund: $33,000 for their performalogue series at the Galería de la Raza. From the art commission of the City of San Francisco, they have a grant to do a series of posters along Market Street. When John filed his tax report for the year 2000, his income sources came from nine different places, which is a good indication that an artist needs to be a businessperson in addition to being a cultural worker and creator of images.

"I think it's really important, especially in this economy, that artists get paid," John says. "It is so common, particularly for muralists, for community artists, that people expect you to do work for free. We put in time volunteering, but I hear it so many times: 'We want you to do a mural.' Is there any money? 'No, well maybe we can get sixty dollars for paints.' And so there's this assumption that this creative work can be done, should be done, and is done for free in our culture. And we don't really have an institution that supports it. It's a cultural assumption." The issue of valuing artists and paying them is particularly crucial in San Francisco, a city with a rich cultural tradition but also the highest cost of living in the country.

John's wife, Aurora, has been teaching bilingual education in a first-grade classroom. Her income helps considerably, since it is regular and dependable, which an artist's income frequently is not.

When asked what advice he has for young artists, John emphasizes the need to redefine what an artist is. "We're not just painters or photographers or media artists," he says. "I think it's really important that you get involved in the community. And that you have some sort of support and network which is close to you and close to your culture and social structure and economic structure. So you don't feel that you're all alone there, and feel that you have to give up your art work to get a nine-to-five job. If you have friends who are artists, if you have a community base which is made up of cultural workers, of activists, of all these other people, then you can find ways in which you can survive, make money, and do your art work."

Araceli Mendoza

Salon Owner

Araceli Mendoza's salon, Karla's Hair Care, is large and bright and bustling, with customers getting manicures, pedicures, shampoos, haircuts, coloring, and permanents from stylists in smart black-and-white smocks patterned with scissor designs. Everything is light and clean and well organized. Conversations and chatter in both Spanish and English, the buzz of clippers, laughter, and the ringing of the telephone blend with pleasant music—classic rock, but not too loud—on the sound system. Araceli, slender and trim with brisk movements as she concentrates on blow-drying a client's hair, works at the station nearest the phone. She frequently pauses to answer it and make appointments.

Everything about the salon is the result of determination and hard work, and of careful and intelligent choices. The location is good—across the street from a large supermarket and in a shopping plaza with a fast-food restaurant, several businesses, and office complexes—in a prosperous, ethnically mixed middle-class neighborhood. The name Karla, Araceli's daughter's name, was chosen because it is a familiar name in both Spanish and English, while English speakers sometimes have trouble with the name Araceli.

Araceli was born in Guadalajara in 1962. Her father, Benito Nadal, worked as a supervisor for the Carta Blanca beer company, which had a policy of transferring their supervisors to a different location every five years. When she was two years old, the family moved to Vera Cruz. "I remember that we used to be in underwear because the heat was terrible. Hot, hot, hot!" she says. "We were there until I was seven, and then we moved to Tepic."

Araceli has two sisters and a brother. Her sister Georgina is older than she is; her brother, Mauricio, is two years younger; and the second sister, Gabriela, is eight years younger. The children all went to Catholic schools. Araceli has good memories of Tepic—of the school, which she liked; of nuns with whom she had close relationships; of volleyball games with her friends. She was in sixth grade and just getting interested in boys when her parents told her the family would be moving again, this time to Zamora in Michoacán.

"It was fine, but I was upset because we moved," she remembers. "But it was a nice town." While they were in Michoacán, her father retired from the Carta Blanca company and opened his own liquor store, so the family stayed there for 14 years. Araceli went to a very good Catholic school called Patria. She got good grades without much studying, and confesses that she used to be a bit wild, at least in the nuns' opinion.

On her 16th birthday her friends asked her mother if they could throw a party—which meant that someone would bring soda and that was a party. Toward the end of the evening, Araceli was explaining to a boy that she didn't want to go with him anymore when she saw an older boy, a very handsome boy, come in with some friends. "I liked the way he looked," she remembers, "but not the way he talked. I thought he was conceited. He used to be very popular." It was Enrique Mendoza, the young man who would become her husband two years later.

Meanwhile Araceli left the Catholic school and went to a public school, which she says was the worst one in the city. Her father would take her there and pick her up afterward. In 1981 she got married. "I got married to get out of my house," she remembers, "and

there we were with his family. We were in the living room with just a mattress on the floor. He had two sisters, and one of them I didn't get along with. A lot of things happened in just a short time."

One of the things that happened was Araceli's first daughter, also named Araceli, was born the following year. Enrique farmed with his father, growing strawberries and watermelons. His family had been moving back and forth from Mexico to the United States since the 1950s, working their own land in Michoacán and doing fieldwork in California.

The year following the birth of their first daughter was extremely difficult for the young couple. Enrique's family, formerly quite prosperous, was having a difficult time and moved to California. Enrique felt that he needed to go with them, but Araceli refused and convinced him to go to her family, now back in Vera Cruz where her father had been offered another job. She was sure her family would be able to find work for her husband, but it was hard because he had no education. He was very depressed—for him it was as though his world had ended. Finally he left Araceli and their daughter with her family and moved to the United States.

"It was a very, very hard time for me," Araceli remembers. "My dad and my mom got too attached to my daughter, and my sister Gabriela—she had been like the princess of the house—got very jealous and she used to say to me, 'Go away. This is not your home. You have your husband.' At that time, if I could have had a place with my family, I never would have come here. Not because of the country, but because of the situation."

Her husband kept telling her to come to the United States, but she was afraid of problems with immigration, and she didn't know any English. Finally Enrique called to say he had the tickets and she needed to come. She knew that she had chosen to get married, and that it wouldn't be good for her daughter to stay with her family, so she took the plane to Tijuana. Her husband was waiting for her with her brother-in-law and some other people.

"My husband had a green card, but we were illegal, my daughter and me," she says. "My husband's family had a birth certificate for a little kid, so they took my daughter with them. And I had my sister-in-law's papers, because she was born here. I told them to go first, because if I saw that they crossed, then I'd have to do it. But if I saw they stopped my daughter, then I wasn't going to do it."

Even though the woman with the birth certificate was very dark, and Araceli's daughter was blond with green eyes, there was no problem. When Araceli got to the border agent, he spoke to her in English because she had a birth certificate. Her husband tried to answer the questions for her, and the agent got upset and sent her to the investigation department. There another agent spoke with her, this time in Spanish, and finally allowed her to go through. "So, miles later, I had my daughter with me, and we'd made it. For me it was like a sign," she says. "I'd said to myself that if I didn't make it, I wouldn't try again. But we made it. And I'm still here."

Enrique worked in the strawberry fields, and they lived in a converted garage in Oxnard, California. There was no insulation, so it was cold in winter and hot in summer, but at least it was a place of their own. The third month after they arrived, Enrique's aunt found Araceli a baby-sitting job to which she could take her daughter while she worked. She was working for a couple who owned a restaurant, and even though she couldn't speak English and didn't understand what the children were saying when they asked for something, she managed.

Her second daughter, Karla, was born in 1985, and her son, Enrique Jr., in 1987. And then she started beauty school.

"There were two schools," she remembers, "one of them Spanish and the other one only English. I went to the English school because I was in America and I wasn't going to work with only Spanish-speaking people. Sometimes when I came home, I hadn't known a word they were talking about the whole day. I didn't know what a comb was." She met two women who were bilingual, who are still her friends, and they helped her. Sometimes she would try so hard to understand that she'd have a headache. "I was ready to quit," she says, "but I said, 'No, I'm going to make it!'"

She graduated from beauty school in 1990, and the doctor told her she was pregnant again. That was a shock because she had planned to start working, and she couldn't. She did have a lot of friends she could practice on, so she would fix their hair. Her best friend in particular was her guinea pig. She says, "I cut her hair, I curled it, I put it every color you can imagine."

Denise, her third daughter, was born in 1991, and six months later Araceli began working in a beauty shop. The clientele at that first shop was mostly older women, so perms and rollers were in demand. After two years Araceli moved to another salon where there were more male clients and younger people. That's where she learned how to work with clippers.

"I learned a lot from both places," she says. "I saw a lot of things. In the first place I learned the things you're not supposed to do, and in the second place the things you are supposed to do. So it was a good experience because I could compare. When I found out I liked it a lot, I wanted to be my own boss. Owning my own shop was always my goal."

She planned for a year, and when she saw the construction starting in the location she wanted, she and her husband went to talk to the building owners. "We didn't know anything," she says. "We didn't even know that we had to have a business license." The owner checked the Mendozas' credit and said he would work with them. They signed the lease in August 1995, and the salon opened in February 1996.

They had a little money and they borrowed on credit cards. They were able to find used furniture and fixtures and equipment that was in excellent condition.

Araceli worked for 45 days by herself, seven days a week, staying open from 9:00 A.M. until 7:00 P.M. Enrique would come to the shop when he got off work, bringing the kids. They would also come on Sundays and spend the day with her. It took a full year before the shop started making any money.

"The growth hasn't been steady," she says. "The first year was the worst. I couldn't find people to work because they didn't think I was going to make it. There weren't too many customers, and stylists lose clients when they move." By 1999 business began improving, and in 2000 the salon grossed $130,000. "Now I have very good people working here. I have very strong people behind me, and that makes a big difference."

Managing employees has been the biggest difficulty Araceli faced in the process of beginning her successful business. "Managing people is the worst thing you can imagine," she says. "I don't have trouble with clients, but dealing with five employees with five different minds . . . and everybody says that I have a chicken heart. But that's the way I am. Sometimes I can be very, very mad, but I can't say anything."

Through hard-won experience, Araceli has learned a more successful approach to working with her staff than she had at the beginning. "Don't try to be friends with your employees," she says. "When you're working, you're working. You can't mix work and friendship. They think in their favor and I think in mine. You need to have your distance. And they respect me. If you want respect, you have to respect them."

When asked what advice she has for someone thinking of starting a business, Araceli emphasized the need for planning. "Think twice," she says, "and then think again. Be sure that it's something that you really want to do." She is sure that she made the right decision in setting her salon up to be bilingual. "That's one of the things here. I have people who speak English, people who speak Spanish. They both feel welcome here. A lot of people say that they like it."

Esperanza Porras-Field

Founder and Owner, Hope and Season Corporation

Esperanza Porras-Field comes from a family of extraordinarily active people. She was born in Bogotá, Colombia, in 1954. Her father was a colonel in the Colombian Army and was also an industrial chemist with a business called Laboratorio Porvi that produced cleaning products such as window cleaners.

"The first time I asked my father for money," Esperanza remembers, "he said, 'You got to go and sell my product, and then you get your money.' That was when I learned how to sell." Her father explained that the Porvi product did four things: It cleaned, disinfected, polished, and shined. With that he sent her off to the nearest gasoline station. She memorized the four functions of the product and approached the first driver who came into the station, saying, "You want to buy the Porvi product?" When the motorist asked what it was, she not only recited what she had learned, but she took a little cloth and cleaned the car. The motorist bought the product for five pesos.

Esperanza's mother had 12 children, six girls and six boys. After she finished raising the last one she went back to school and became a journalist, a lawyer, a psychologist, and then a diplomat representing Colombia internationally. This remarkable woman was 90 years old in 2000, living in the United States and studying every day for the U.S. citizenship test, which she was to take in 2001. "She's very optimistic," Esperanza says. "She never thinks that anything is going to go wrong. Everything is going to go right. So I guess we got the positive way of both of them. I think you become an entrepreneur because your family is into this."

Esperanza and her brothers and sisters went to military school in Bogotá, which is not like military schools in the United States. In Colombia there is only one kind of military school, and it is for children whose parents are in the military. She started classes in the university, but a strike closed it down, so her father sent her to the United States to learn English and become bilingual. "I failed English all through high school," she says, "so he wanted to punish me and I had to take it. So I was sent to St. Peter's College in New Jersey. My father said, 'You finish there, and then you come back.' But when I was in my last year of school, my father died."

Esperanza was a top student. She began the college program with 80 students from all over the world. They studied in England and Spain as well as in the United States. When her father died, her mother wanted Esperanza to return to Colombia, but by that time she was dating the man who would become her husband, and she didn't want to return. She told her mother that she was staying because she wanted to graduate, which she did in 1979, taking degrees in both social science and political science. She was the only one of the original 80 students to graduate.

Esperanza married as soon as she graduated, and the couple had two daughters. She and her husband separated when her girls were one and three years old. She raised the girls herself and at the same time started her own company. "Actually, that forced me to become an entrepreneur," she says, "because . . . nobody would take me if I said I had to drive my daughter back and forth, or she's sick with the chicken pox. I had a real estate license—the first thing I did when I was in college was to get a real estate license."

She decided to start her own real estate company, which she did; she owned that company for 14 years. She had 21 sales associates and learned how to be her own broker.

At the same time she was taking classes at Smith University in Rhode Island, studying all types of training techniques. She received a master's degree and for five years, from 1990 to 1995, worked for the New Jersey Highway Authority as their training manager. She designed and implemented the training for toll collectors, engineers, secretaries—all of the highway authority employees. Meanwhile, she ran her real estate business.

When her daughters became teenagers, however, she sold her business. As she put it, "I needed to put my eye where the action is," and the action was at home. Another factor in her decision was the death of a brother she loved very much who was living in Germany. He had frequently invited her to come over to visit him, but she always told him she was too busy—she had to go to school and she had to take care of her company. When he died, she sold her company and made all the funeral arrangements for him.

"So that was painful for me," she remembers. "Nothing is worth it in this life more than having the things that you want to do when you want to do them." She took her daughters and traveled all over Europe with them for a month and a half in 1995. When the family returned from Europe, Esperanza became an associate with Coldwell Banker, the big real estate company to which she had sold her company. She kept her company name, however, for the consulting company she started next.

As a consultant she operates in several areas. She is a real estate consultant, a training consultant, and now a television consultant as well, since she produces her own television show. The show is called *Mi casa es su casa (My House Is Your House)* and is the only bilingual show in the United States. "If you speak Spanish," Esperanza says, "we speak Spanish. If you speak English, we speak English. If you speak Spanglish, we speak Spanglish. People come to the show and we do interviews. It's a one-hour show, divided into different modules: community issues, business, sports and recreation, and entertainment."

The show is on the air every Saturday at 5:00 P.M. Esperanza is the producer and does one of the interview segments. She has 26 people working as volunteers, four hostesses and two directors among them. "Sometimes I don't do any of the segments and let the others do them. This is a voluntary show. If somebody doesn't show up, I do it. This is something I do free for the community." For profit, she acts as an agent selling entertainment. If someone needs a piano player, she knows whom to contact. If someone needs to make a videotape, she has those contacts in the media.

For the training part of the business, she has different trainers. For instance, if AT&T requests sexual harassment training, Esperanza has a person who specializes in that kind of training, according to her standards. She leases out the trainers to the companies that need them, working as an agent. Sometimes she does trainings herself.

Esperanza married again in 1998, to Juan Carlos Garcia, who has his own import and export business and also works with her. "The main corporation remains the same," Esperanza explains, "Hope and Season. I mainly concentrate on the real estate and my husband and kids do the other part. So that's why the company is called Hope and Season. Everybody is hoping to do a deal in the right season. Some things are good in the winter, some things are good in the spring."

By far the largest source of Esperanza's income is her real estate consulting. In real estate she belongs to the Million Dollar Club—she sold $25 million worth of real estate in the year 2000.

"A consultant is when you're selling your mind, your knowledge," she says. "For instance, if the bank and the community are doing a joint venture for the Community Rehabilitation Act, they need someone who knows how to put it together. If the deal costs $400,000, I get paid a percentage as a consultant . . . telling them how to put it together, how to do it. You kind of draw the map."

As a part of her consulting business, she is frequently called upon to advise people who want to start their own business. "The first thing they should do is a business plan," she says, "because without a business plan you most likely will fail. That's the first thing to do, because in the process of doing a business plan you're going to find out who's your competition. You have to do financial planning. The business plan should be for a minimum of five

years. The first five years are going to be difficult. And there's not really going to be a lot of profit."

Another thing Esperanza stresses is that people should go into a business that they like and know. "The majority of people, they come to me with ideas, but they don't know what they're talking about. For instance, a woman came to me wanting to open a restaurant, and I said, 'Do you know how to cook?'

"And she said, 'No.'

"I said, 'Did you ever work for a business that had a restaurant?'

"And she said, 'No.'

"I said, 'Why do you want to open a restaurant?'

"She said, 'Because somebody offered it to me.'

"So I said, 'Do you have a budget?'

"She said, 'No'

"'How are you going to get the money?'

"'I want to get a second mortgage on my house.'

"I said, 'Are you out of your mind? Are you crazy?'

"So she got very upset with me. She said, 'You're my friend. You're supposed to advise me well. It seems to me that you're jealous of me.'

"I said, 'Because I care for you, I'm telling you that you're making the wrong decision. This is not what business is about.'

"It's like me opening a mechanic shop when I don't know anything about mechanics. So the main thing is for people to know what they're doing, to have experience in what they're doing, and have a good business financial plan. Once you do that, you'll see a lot. And a business plan is not something you do in two days. It takes at least six months or more."

Esperanza Porras-Field does so many things that it would make most people dizzy just trying to remember them all, much less do them. "I accomplish a lot," she says. "I get up early. I have an appointment book. And I keep my appointments. I even make appointments to do my own laundry. Or to read a book. Or to read to be prepared for a meeting. I have to read my material. I am a professor at Fairleigh Dickinson University in Madison, New Jersey—the same university where my daughter goes to school. I teach one class. I have to prepare my papers for my students. I have to give myself time to do that."

In addition to her very busy business activities, Esperanza is also in-volved in politics and community service. She is the vice president of the Democratic Party in Morristown. She ran for freeholder and got 50,000 votes in a county that was completely Republican, proving the point that she could get votes. She began the Hispanic Chamber of Commerce in her county and has been its president three times.

With all this, she makes sure that she spends time with her family. They have dinner together every night. "And we go to church on Sunday," she says. "I have a family day. We have respect for each other, and we're very happy." She is also physically active. She likes swimming and was a champion swimmer when she was younger. She currently belongs to a gym and likes walking two or three miles. "The main thing in life is health," she says. "If you've got good health, you've got it all."

Mabel Tinjacá, Ph.D.

Author and Consultant in Organizational Development

Mabel Tinjacá was born in Bogotá, Colombia, exactly at noon on May 30, 1953. She was the youngest of three children and the only girl. Her father's name was Heriberto Tinjacá. "My dad was a very intelligent man," she remembers, "one of those people who have so many talents they can't quite figure out which one to nurture." At one point he had been a matador. He had also been a pharmacist and taught English at a university.

Mabel's mother, Clara Inez Vargas, was the second of 12 children and the oldest girl. A small woman, she was the first in her family to go to college—where she played basketball even though she was only five feet tall—and earned a degree in accounting. The Vargas family had been quite wealthy at one time, but Mabel's grandfather had lost most of his fortune. Clara's aunts and uncles helped her through college.

"My parents were not a match made in heaven," Mabel says, "but my mom the eternal romantic was enchanted with a handsome matador who happened to be very intelligent." After Mabel's father had tried out a few ca-reers in Colombia, he received a schol-arship to medical school in the United States and moved the family to New York City for a while, where they did quite well. Mabel remembers living in a beautiful three-story house in Queens, where she had a spacious room on the third floor with a closet big enough to be her playhouse.

From that comfortable lifestyle, Mabel and her mother and brothers were plunged into poverty when her parents divorced, and her mother moved them to Spanish Harlem. Her father went back to Colombia. "We didn't telephone; I assume we could not afford it. We soon lost track of him," Mabel says. "Letter writing was not going to do it for me at five."

Mabel went to public schools, first in Spanish Harlem and then in Black Harlem. She says that she owes a lot to P.S. 39, which had fabulous school pro-grams. On Wednesdays the city would take any student who needed dental care to the dentist. This is where she had her first exposure to dentistry. "But it wasn't only that," she says. "We vis-ited Carnegie Hall and the World's Fair I can't tell you how many times. We got to go to Lincoln Center, where we heard classical music and opera. The cultural experience that was afforded through that public school was extraordinary."

When Mabel was 14, her mother remarried. Mabel's stepfather, Ramón Pagán, was from Puerto Rico. He moved the family from New York City to Lorain, Ohio, where there was a small Puerto Rican community. When Mabel and her brothers were teenagers, their stepfather set up an upholstering shop in their home. "I'm appreciating him more as I get older," Mabel says. "I went through my teen years and I did what teenagers do, I rebelled and gave him a hard time."

Like many expatriates, Ramón Pagán felt the call of his homeland. He decided it was time for the family to live where they could speak Spanish and could understand the culture. This was very hard for Mabel. Even though Spanish was her first language, at that point she was predominantly an English speaker, and all her education had been in English. She did not want to go to Puerto Rico, but they went. She quickly learned to love the "Island of Enchantment" and its warmhearted people. She graduated from high school there and entered the University of Puerto Rico when she was 17.

In 1974, when she was 21, she received a bachelor's degree in psychology from the University of Puerto Rico.

After graduation, Mabel Tinjacá went back to New York and took a job "to pay the bills" in the customer service department of an insurance company; later she became a consultant to the City of New York. She applied to several behavioral psychology graduate programs and was accepted at the University of Kansas, her first choice because of its excellent faculty. "I worked to fund my education," she says, "at least half-time and sometimes three quarters of the time. Since I worked the entire time, it just dragged it out forever. I was teaching, and I was doing a lot of school consulting for the university."

When asked to describe what a consultant does, Mabel explained that a good consultant is much like a teacher: A consultant provides information. If the client needs to make a decision, the consultant provides the facts, the options, and how best to get to the client's goal. She sees consulting as a process of supporting developmental processes. These developmental processes are her primary interest. She received her

Ph.D. in 1983 in applied behavioral analysis and developmental psychology.

Like many entrepreneurs, Mabel combined running her own business with working within large corporations. She was an internal consultant for AlliedSignal, Inc., now Honeywell, Inc., in Kansas City, an aerospace company with interests in automotive and engineered materials. This allowed her to work nationally with the other Allied companies as well as with the U.S. Department of Energy. "I was working in organization development," she says. "This thread of development is very clear for me. I worked with children in classrooms, then adults in education, managers and executives, and then systems within complex organizations." Behavioral psychology studies the environmental factors that affect the performance of individuals as well as the performance of organizations.

One of her fondest memories in working in manufacturing, Mabel recalls, is of when she and an innovative production team superimposed a business unit structure so that the group could see themselves as a stand-alone business rather than just an anonymous part of a huge corporation. "It allowed the team and each person to show their capabilities," she says. One group had production problems resulting from the perceived and actual status of the different workers: engineers were considered most important, and the hourly workers who assembled the product had the lowest status. Needless to say, communication within the groups was poor.

Tinjacá worked at AlliedSignal until 1993. She received several service awards and was promoted to manager of organization development—she was the second woman to become a manager, which was quite significant in a male-oriented engineering corporation. She was at a point where she began thinking, "Where am I going, and what's my next step? I decided that I really do have an entrepreneurial soul, and I needed to test that out."

She began working with the Kauffman Center for Entrepreneurial Leadership at the Ewing Marion Kauffman Foundation in Kansas City. She became more and more fascinated with fast-growth entrepreneurs who start companies and then go big. About that time Mabel married William Tucker, and in 1995 they had a child, Christopher. "He's very much a Midwesterner," she says about her husband, "with a very solid family. He's in sales, equipment for large construction projects, and is one of the top sales people in his company."

Between 1992 and 1995, Mabel married, changed jobs, purchased a home, and became a parent. All of these changes caused her to take stock. It was time for her to give back to her community. She had worked hard in school, done corporate work, and managed to run her own consulting business. When she started thinking of ways that she could give back to the Hispanic community, a friend suggested that she write a book about Hispanic entrepreneurs. Writing would mean that she would spend more time at home with her son.

"This was in 1997," she says. "I loved the idea, but I imagined that book had already been written. I was intrigued. I thought, 'Wow, what if it hasn't been written?'" She asked the library to search for books on the topic. "Except for two regional books, one in New Orleans and one in Texas, there wasn't such a book."

It took Mabel Tinjacá three years of exhausting long nights and difficult research to complete her project. The information about Hispanic entrepreneurs needed to be gathered from Hispanic Chambers of Commerce nation-

ally. At that point the data about Hispanic businesses was scarce. Information was available, mostly in two magazines, *Hispanic Business* and *Hispanic Magazine*. *Hispanic Business* lists the top 500 Hispanic businesses in their June issue each year. This was very helpful. Then Tinjacá developed a network to get businesspeople to agree to be interviewed.

"I started reading newspapers and magazine articles about people and what they were doing," she says. "I called around. I used the Internet. One interview led to another interview led to another interview. Eventually I had thirty interviews and I had to select six for the first book. Researching this way was the equivalent of pounding the pavement on the computer and the telephone."

Mabel discovered things about entrepreneurs that she thinks anyone seriously considering starting their own company should think about. One thing that the people she interviewed have in common is that they are in love with the whole process of learning and growth—lifelong learning is essential to them. They go out of their way to learn. Not all of them finished high school, but they are avid learners. She thinks, however, that education will be more and more necessary in building companies: "Our society continues to become more sophisticated, business owners will need formal education to, for instance, compete for venture capital funding and to manage mergers and acquisitions. Although I continue to run into people who don't have extensive education and do very well, I believe they are very talented and gifted people. The rest of us need to finish school and perhaps specialize."

Tinjacá found that recent Latino immigrants are doing very well as business owners. "I think you have to know yourself very well," she says, "what your strengths are and what your weaknesses are. If you are really interested in being an entrepreneur, you have to put together a *winning package.* You learn to shore up your weaknesses by either bringing in a partner or bringing the right people into the organization so that you can work to your strengths."

She suggests that it is a good idea to have experience working in the industry you are considering. "Learn the business for a few years as an employee. Be willing to work very, very hard for a long time. It may not pay off right away. You have to have persistence."

Mabel Tinjacá 's book, *¡Vision! Hispanic Entrepreneurs in the United States,* was published by Heritage Publishing Company in 2001 and has received excellent reviews. She continued to grow her consulting business as she wrote *¡Vision!* "There are a lot of intangibles in writing," she says. "You clarify your thoughts, both about the topic and about yourself. You meet wonderful people."

Her business is fundamentally a practice that offers consulting services to corporations, to high-growth entrepreneurs, and to nonprofit organizations. "In a business like this," she says, "you can make any amount of money you set your sights on. It can be very lucrative, but it means very hard work. I specialize in facilitation, strategic planning, and leadership development in companies that are growing very fast." Certainly she is finding that the Hispanic community is a place where many such companies are found.

PART
3

Resources

Books

Starting a Business

Bangs, David H. *The Start-up Guide: A One-Year Plan for Entrepreneurs.* Dover, NH: Upstart Publishing Co., 1994.

Caplan, Suzanne. *A Piece of the Action: How Women and Minorities Can Launch Their Own Successful Businesses.* New York: American Management Association, 1994.

Dyer, W. Gibb, Jr. *The Entrepreneurial Experience: Confronting the Career Dilemmas of the Start-up Executive.* San Francisco: Jossey-Bass Publishers, 1992.

Fallek, Max. *Finding Money for Your Small Business.* Dearborn, MI: Enterprise, 1994.

Friedman, Robert L. *The Entrepreneur's Sourcebook.* San Diego: Wescomm Services, Inc., 1999.

Gonzalez, Charles, J. Reichert, and P. Caldwell. *Yes You Can! Every Latino's Guide to Building Family Wealth.* Worchester, MA: Chandler House Press, 1998.

Kanellos, Nicolas. *Hispanic Firsts: 500 Years of Extraordinary Achievement.* Houston, TX: Arte Público Press, 1997.

Koch, Harry Walter. *A California Small Business Handbook.* Berkeley, CA: Ken-Books, 1993.

Leska, Matthew. *Free Money to Change Your Life.* Kensington, MD: Information USA, Inc., 1999.

———. *Government Giveaways for Entrepreneurs.* Kensington, MD: Information USA, Inc., 1996.

Mancuso, Joseph R. *How to Get a Business Loan Without Signing Your Life Away.* New York: Simon & Schuster, 1993.

Nicholas, Ted. *How to Form Your Own Corporation Without a Lawyer for under $75.* Wilmington, DE: Enterprise Publishing, 1999.

Pinson, Linda, and Jerry Jinnett. *The Home-Based Entrepreneur.* Dover, NH: Upstart Publishing Co., 1993.

Rodriguez, Gregory. *The Emerging Latino Middle Class.* Malibu, CA: Pepperdine University Institute for Public Policy, 1996.

Sexton, Donald L., and N. Bowman-Upton. *Entrepreneurship: Creativity and Growth.* New York: McMillan, 1991.

Small Business Administration. *Hispanic-Owned Businesses and the SBA: Outreach Initiatives-Hispanic Fact Sheet.* Washington, D.C.: Small Business Administration, 1999.

Sundt, Peter C. *Business Start-up Handbook: Guidelines and Pitfalls.* Houston, TX: Cibolo Press, 1999.

Timmons, Jeffry A. *New Venture Creation: Entrepreneurship for the 21st Century.* New York: McGraw-Hill Higher Education, 1999.

Tinjacá, Mabel. *¡Vision! Hispanic Entrepreneurs in the United States.* Pleasant Hill, MO: Heritage Publishing Co., 2001.

Buying a Business

Bazerman, Max H., and Margaret A. Neale. *Negotiating Rationally.* New York: The Free Press, 1993.

Bumstead, William W. *Buying and Selling Businesses.* New York: John Wiley & Sons, 1998.

Fifer, Bob. *Double Your Profits in 6 Months or Less.* New York: Harper Business, 1994.

Freund, James C. *Smart Negotiating.* New York: Simon & Schuster, 1993.

Gabriel, Colin. *How to Sell Your Business—And Get What You Want!* Westport, CT: Gwent Press, 1998.

Goldfarb, Steven G. *Selling Your Business: Beat the Sharks at Their Own Game When You Cash Out.* Chicago: North Harbor Press, 2001.

McGregor, Ronald J. *Buying a Business.* Menlo Park, CA: Crisp Publications, Inc., 1993.

Marren, Joseph H. *Mergers and Acquisitions—A Valuation Handbook.* New York: McGraw-Hill Professional Publishing, 1992.

Nattonson, Ira N. *The Secrets of Buying and Selling a Business.* Grants Pass, OR: The Oasis Press, 1994.

Post, Alexandra M. *Anatomy of a Merger.* Englewood Cliffs, NJ: Prentice Hall, 1994.

Rickertsen, Rick, Robert E. Gunther, and Michael Lewis. *Buyout: The Insider's Guide to Buying Your Own Company.* New York: AMACOM Books, 2001.

Robb, Russell. *Buying Your Own Business.* Holbrook, MA: Adams Publishing, 1995.

Snowden, Richard W. *The Complete Guide to Buying a Business.* New York: AMACOM Books, 1993.

Weston, J. Fred. *Mergers and Acquisitions.* New York: McGraw-Hill Professional Publishing, 2001.

Franchising

Barkoff, Rupert M. *The Fundamentals of Franchising.* Chicago: American Bar Association, 1997.

Braddock, Jeffrey L. *Franchise Organizations.* Boston: Harvard Business School, 1998.

Dugan, Ann, editor. *Franchising 101: The Complete Guide to Evaluating, Buying and Growing Your Franchised Business.* Dover, NH: Upstart Publishing Company, 1998.

Foster, Dennis L. *Franchising for Free: Owning Your Own Business Without Investing Your Own Cash.* New York: John Wiley & Sons, 1988.

Kahn, Mahmood A. *Restaurant Franchising.* New York: John Wiley & Sons, 1999.

Lashley, Conrad, and Alison Morrison, editors. *Franchising Hospitality Industry.* Oxford, UK: Butterworth-Heinemann, 2000.

McCallum, Ross A. *Franchising: An Accounting, Auditing, and Income Tax Guide.* New York: John Wiley & Sons, 1993.

Mendelsohn, Martin. *The Guide to Franchising.* London: Cassell Academic, 1999.

Patel, Jay. *Franchising: Is It Fair? How to Negotiate an Equitable Franchise Agreement.* Rochester, IL: WeWrite Corp., 1999.

Perry, Robert L. *The 50 Best Low-Investment, High-Profit Franchises.* Englewood Cliffs, NJ: Prentice Hall, 1994.

Rule, Roger C. *No Money Down: Financing for Franchising.* Central Point, OR: P.S.I. Research–Oasis Press, 1998.

Sherman, Andrew J. *Franchising and Licensing: Two Ways to Build Your Business.* New York: AMACOM Books, 1999.

Shook, Carrie, and Robert L. Shook. *Franchising: The Business Strategy that Changed the World.* Englewood Cliffs, NJ: Prentice Hall, 1993.

Thomas, Dave, and Michael Seid. *Franchising for Dummies.* New York: Hungry Minds, Inc., 2000.

Internet Sources

Starting a Business

American Export Register: www.aernet.com/English

Barron's Online: www.barrons.com

Business Web Page: www.bizweb.com

The CCH Business Owner's Toolkit: www.toolkit.cch.com

The Center for Business Planning: www.businessplans.org

Companies Online: www.companiesonline.com

Consumer Price Indexes on the
Internet: stats.bls.gov/
cpihome.htm

Consumer's Independent Guide to
Small Business Insurance:
www.kpia.com/consumer/
Consbiz.html

Dun & Bradstreet Patent
Information:
www.aol.telebase.com/
mpatents.htm

Entrepreneurial Edge:
www.edgeonline.com

EntreWorld, "A World of Resources
for Entrepreneurs":
www.entreworld.org

Finding Money for Your Small
Business: www.garage.com

Harris Information Source
(American manufacturers):
www.harrisinfo.com

IBM Patent Server:
www.patents.ibm.com

Inc.: www.inc.com

Insurance Information Institute:
www.iii.org

Internal Revenue Service:
www.irs.ustreas.gov/prod

MoneyHunt, "The Proven Path to
Capital":
www.moneyhunter.com

Service Corps of Retired
Executives (SCORE):
www.score.org

Small Businesses Online
Resource: www.smalloffice.com

The Thomas Register of Industrial
Products and Services:
www.thomasregister.com

U.S. Department of Commerce:
www.doc.gov

U.S. Patent and Trademark Office:
www.uspto.gov

U.S. Small Business
Administration: www.sba.gov

The Wall Street Journal:
www.wsj.com

Working Solo:
www.workingsolo.com

Workz Tips: www.workz.com

Buying a Business

Business Web Page:
www.bizweb.com

The Fortt Guide to Buying and
Selling a Business:
www.bizbuysale.com

Service Corps of Retired
Executives (SCORE):
www.score.org

Franchising

Advanced Franchising Worldwide:
www.afww.com

Be The Boss: www.betheboss.com

Dwyer Group Home Page:
www.dwyergroup.com

Experts in Franchising:
www.expertsinfranchising.com

The Franchise Company:
www.franchising-
consultants.com

Franchise Conxions:
www.franchise-conxions.com

Franchise Net:
www.franchisenet.com

Franchise Times:
www.franchisetimes.com

Franchising Information
Resource: www.franchising.org

Franchising Times:
www.franchisingtimes.com

Guide to International
Franchising:
www.franchiseintl.com

RK Franchise Consultancy:
www.rkfranchise.com

Tricon Global Home Page (KFC,
Pizza Hut, Taco Bell):
www.triconglobal.com

U.S. Franchise Systems, Inc.:
www.usfsi.com

Master Index to Careers

actor/actress, En

acupuncturist, SM

administrative assistant, CS, Ed

advertising copywriter, En

advertising salesperson, PC

agent, En, Sp, MI

agriculturalist, SM

alternative medical practitioner, SM

ambassador, LP

animator, En

archaeologist, SM

art director, PC

associate director, nonprofit organization, CS

astronomer, SM

athlete, professional, Sp

athletic director, Sp

athletic trainer, Sp

attorney *see* lawyer

bailiff, LP

baseball umpire, Sp

biologist, SM

board member, CS

broadcast engineer, PC

broadcaster *see also* journalist, CS

bus driver, Ed

business owner, LE

casting director, En

chemist, SM

chief executive officer/executive director/president, CS, LE

chiropractor, SM

choreographer, En

cinematographer (director of photography), En

city administrator, LP

classified worker, Ed

coach/manager, Ed, Sp

columnist, PC

comedian, En

comedy writer, En

communications/media relations/ public relations officer, CS

community affairs director (television), En

composer, En, MI

computer engineer, Tc

computer programmer, Tc

computer technician, Tc

conductor, MI

copyeditor, PC

copywriter, PC

costume designer (theater/ television/film), En

court reporter, LP

crime prevention specialist, LP

criminal defense lawyer, LP

critic/reviewer, En, MI

KEY
CS—Community Service
Ed—Education
En—Entertainment
LE—Latino Entrepreneurs
LP—Law and Politics
MI—Music Industry
PC—Publishing and Communications
SM—Science and Medicine
Sp—Sports
Tc—Technology

data base manager, Tc
data entry clerk, Tc
data processing technician, Tc
dental hygienist, SM
dentist, SM
director (feature films or television), En
disc jockey/radio announcer, PC, MI
editor, PC
engineer, SM
engineering technician, SM
equipment manager, Sp
FBI agent, LP
film editor, En
fingerprint expert, LP
football referee, Sp
foreign service officer, LP
forester, SM
founder, CS, LE
fund-raiser for nonprofit organization, CS
general manager (station manager), PC
geologist, SM
government relations officer, LP
grant writer, CS
graphic designer, PC, Tc
graphics programmer, Tc
guidance counselor, Ed
home health care worker, CS
human rights worker, LP
immigration and customs officer, LP
instructional assistant, Ed
instrumental musician, MI
journalist, CS, En, LP, PC, Sp, MI
judge, LP
justice of the peace, LP

juvenile detention officer, LP
labor representative (organizer, regional director), CS
laboratory technician, SM
lawyer (attorney, paralegal), CS, En, LP, Sp
legal secretary, LP
librarian, Ed
lighting designer (theater), En
makeup artist (theater/television/film), En
manufacturer's representative, Sp
marketing director, Sp
medical doctor, CS, SM
medical scientist, SM
meteorologist/weather forecaster, PC, SM
music librarian, MI
music teacher, MI
news director, PC
news writer (radio), PC
notary public, LP
nurse, CS, SM
nutritionist, SM
optometrist, SM
paramedic, emergency medical technician (EMT), SM
parole officer, LP
personal trainer, Sp
pharmacist, SM
photographer or camera operator, PC
physical therapist, SM
physician, SM
physicist, SM
playwright, En
podiatrist, SM
police officer, LP
political lobbyist, LP
political strategist, LP

politician, LP
press agent, En
principal, Ed
probation officer, LP
producer, En, MI
professional scout, Sp
professor, college or university, Ed
program director, PC
promoter, music and events, MI
proofreader, PC
psychiatrist, SM
psychologist, Ed, SM
public relations director, En, PC,
    Sp
publicist, Sp
publicity director, PC
publisher, PC
radio producer, PC
recording engineer, MI
recording technician, MI
representative (Congress), LP
retail manager or clerk, MI
sales representative (books), PC
scenic designer (theater), En
science technician, SM
screenwriter, En
senator, LP
set designer (theater/television/
    film/video), En
singer, MI
sound editor, En
sound technician, MI
sports reporter/sportscaster, PC,
    Sp
stage director, En
stage manager, En
superintendent (school), Ed
systems analyst, Tc
teacher, Ed
    technical support specialist, Tc

technical writer, PC
television news anchor, PC
tour publicist, En
tuner, musical instruments, MI
translator/interpreter, LP
treaty negotiator, LP
veterinarian, SM
victim advocate, LP
Web master, Tc
writer, book, PC
youth coordinator, CS

Master Index to People Profiled

Galindo, Max, Paramedic, SM

Garcia, Abraham and Ana Corinna, Business Owners, Computer Company, LE

Garcia, Paul, Web master, Tc

Garcia, Rodolfo, Relationship Banker, LP

Gates, Ann Quiroz, computer science professor, Tc

Girón, Carlos, Sports Publicist, Sp

Gomez, Julio, founder and owner of e-commerce consulting firm, Tc

Gonzales, Enrique, project manager for a network of Web sites, Tc

Gonzales, Thomas, technology consultant, Tc

Gonzales, Victor, computer programmer, Tc

Gonzalez, Alex, Baseball Player, Sp

Guerrero, Lena, Political Lobbyist, LP

Gutiérrez, Margo, Librarian, Ed

Guzman-Macias, Estela, Special Education Teacher, Resource Specialist, Ed

Hayek, Salma Actress, En

Henley, Maria Jimenez, Stage Manager, Assistant Director, Choreographer, and Dancer, En

Hernandez, Antonia, Lawyer, President, CS

Hernandez, Fidel, Zoologist, SM

Hernandez, G. Herb, County Councilman at Large, LP

Hernandez-Castillo, Bel, Publisher, Editor-in-Chief, Dancer, and Actress, En

Herrera, Leticia, Business Owner, Cleaning Service, LE

Heumann, Judith, Assistant Secretary for Special Education, Ed

Jaime, Mental Health Technician, SM

Jimenez, James, City Administrator, LP

Kanellos, Nicolás, Book Publisher, PC

Leanos, John, Cultural Worker, Artist, LE

Leguizamo, John, Actor, Comedian, Playwright, En

Leoni, Dennis Edward, Writer, Producer, En

Llamosa, Carlos, Soccer Player, Sp

Llanes, David, Record Company Owner, MI

Lopez, George, Comedian, En

Los Lobos (David Hidalgo, Conrad Lozano, Louie Perez, and Cesar Rosas), musicians, MI

Martinez, Christine, radio disc jockey, MI

Martinez, Gilbert, Chief Judge, LP

Martinez, Rueben, Bookstore Owner, PC

Martinez, Walter, Magazine Publisher, Editor, PC

Massó, Jose, Center for the Study of Sport in Society, Sp

McBride, Theresa, computer systems consultant, Tc

Index